25 Dec. 93

Merry Christmas
Frank and Karleen,
We've had lots of fun
evenings at Skoshi Room (Jack's place)
watching Sumo and rolling dice
for drinks. I hope this book will always
give you happy memories of Sumo,
Okinawa and our friendship.

Lots of love,
Diana
aka "Chikara"
力 forever

RIKISHI

RIKISHI
The Men of Sumo

by JOEL SACKETT
text by WES BENSON

New York • WEATHERHILL • *Tokyo*

The characters facing the title page read *gomen komuru*, "with honorable permission," and are a legacy of the days when sumo was performed at the leave of the shogunate authorities. In that spirit of gratitude, the authors thank the *rikishi* whose lives are recorded in these pages. The endpapers reproduce handprints (*tegata*) of yokozunas Chiyonofuji and Futahaguro.

FIRST EDITION, 1986

Published by John Weatherhill, Inc., of New York and Tokyo, with editorial offices at 7-6-13 Roppongi, Minato-ku, Tokyo 106, Japan. Protected by copyright under terms of the International Copyright Union; all rights reserved. Printed in Japan.

Library of Congress cataloging in Publication Data: Sackett, Joel. / Rikishi. / 1. Sumo—Japan. 2. Wrestlers—Japan. / I. Benson, Wes. II. Title. / GV1197.S23 1986 796.8'125 86-22368 / ISBN 0-8348-0214-7

In memory of Rahoul

Contents

Color photographs precede the text.

Preface

I knew immediately that I liked sumo. It seemed at once altogether new, yet somehow familiar. Finally, I figured out where the familiarity lay. When I was eleven or twelve years old, my friend's father would take us to the Golden Glove matches at Sunnyside Gardens in New York. In one long evening we would see about thirty or more four-round fights beginning with flyweights and progressing through the various weight limits to the final main heavyweight bout. We always sat near ringside, and the blood and spit would sometimes stain our clothes. The boxers were kids—sixteen, seventeen, eighteen years old—of every ethnic origin New York had to offer. Most of the matches would begin in good form and degenerate into a brawl by the third round. The most exciting sort of match was when a gawky, round-shouldered kid was up against a tough, well-built, cocky opponent. The "sure bet" would be prancing, jabbing, and taunting the "loser," whose only hope seemed to be to protect himself from a slaughter. Then, out of his cocoon the loser would explode with a single knockout punch, and it was all over, bringing the crowd to their feet. That was justice!

As distant and incomparable as the worlds of the boxer and the rikishi are in most ways, a version of the same David-and-Goliath contest is replayed in the sumo ring when a small (250-pound) *rikishi* faces a much larger opponent. Smaller fighters often develop higher degrees of technique, speed, and cunning to offset the sheer mass of their rivals. *Yokozuna* Chiyonofuji, not at all a giant among rikishi, has combined all of these qualities, plus a massive reserve of strength, to stay way ahead of the pack in recent years.

Chiyonofuji was the first rikishi I met, in a setting I will not soon forget. I was introduced to him by Wes Benson (who brought me into the normally closed world of sumo) in a small coffee shop next to the temple where the rikishi of Kokonoe *beya* were staying during the March 1985 Osaka tournament. Chiyonofuji hardly looked up—not because he was aloof, but because he was engrossed in a game of space invaders. Above him on the wall was one of his autographed hand prints, proudly displayed by the proprietor. Several neighborhood people were having coffee; they didn't crowd the yokozuna or pay particular attention to this very special patron. Chiyonofuji was wearing a loose *yukata*. From a few feet away I could see the definition of his arms, chest, and legs. I recall observing that even his toes looked carved from stone. Without raising my camera, I looked over the scene again in monochrome, framing it in several ways. But the light was decidedly against me. I would need a strobe to get anything useful. Would it be worth it, I thought? After all, I had just been introduced minutes ago and was seeking his cooperation on a long-term documentary. There would be other opportunities, and there was no need to disturb him more than I already had—a yokozuna has to face countless cameras and strobes every day. This first meeting was a lesson in restraint, something that all Japanese live with. It was a lesson that would be repeated several times during this project and in other situations working in Japan. I ordered a second cup of coffee and was more than content just to be there.

It was a day of firsts. Later that morning, inside the temple, was my first encounter with sumo family life. All the young rikishi were quietly busy cooking and getting out the morning meal. Huge pots of *chanko nabe* bubbled away on gas burners, with plenty of reserves to replenish the pot. Chiyonofuji and his stablemate Hoshi (who is now *ozeki* Hokutoumi) sat down first with the *oyakata*, hairdresser, and guests. The yokozuna motioned for me to sit at his side—a privileged seat, and one that was offered less and less as I became a fixture around the heya. He poured me a bowl of beer and encouraged me to dig into the pot, which I did. Enough restraint for one day.

That day in March 1985 marks the beginning of this project. I continued photographing through the New Year's tournament of 1986. In addition to attending most of the tournaments in that interval, I was fortunate to be able to accompany the rikishi on their *jungyo* tour to the Hokuriku region. Most of my time with the men of sumo was spent at Kokonoe beya, where I became closest to the rikishi. At first, the young rikishi were very shy. They had never had such close contact with a foreigner before. But, after spending many days and nights with them, sleeping in the same communal room during the Nagoya tournament, sharing the chanko and the bath, hanging my laundry next to theirs, and partying on several *senshuraku* nights, I found my tentative place in their world. There are two members of Kokonoe beya I would especially like to thank: Toshio Inaba, the manager, who kept me posted on events and showed me some of the nightlife on the sumo trail, and Hideyuki Iwaki, who taught me much about sumo etiquette and style. Iwaki-san was the main attendant to Chiyonofuji then; he has since retired and become a coach at Kokonoe beya. I would also like to thank the members of Takasago beya for their cooperation, particularly Konishiki, for the pleasant afternoons I spent with him in the heya. My thanks also go to Kitao—now yokozuna Futahaguro—of Tatsunami beya for his cooperation. The members of Oshima beya were kind to me as well, allowing me to spend several mornings photographing *keiko* practice, and it was there that I also enjoyed a chanko with Asahifuji. A special thanks to Azumazeki (Jesse) Daigoro, who invited me to his home to photograph his topknot, which he keeps encased and on display in his living room since his retirement. I am grateful to the Sumo Kyokai, who allowed me access to the *shitaku beya* and permission to travel on private trains with the rikishi during jungyo.

Outside the sumo world, I would like to thank the Leica distributor in Japan, Nihon Siber Hegner, K.K., for supplying all of the film stock I used and for the use of a Leica M6 and lenses, which (along with a Leica M2) I used exclusively for this project. The Leica rangefinder, with its quiet, low-vibration shutter and excellent lenses, allowed me to work at very low light levels in an unobtrusive manner. The printing paper, Ilford's Ilfospeed and Multigrade II, was generously provided by the Ilford Group Unit of Ciba-Geigy (Japan) Limited. I found these papers and their chemistry very responsive and flexible in making the reproduction prints. Two colleagues, both photographers, helped me to edit several hundred prints: thank you Jerry Burchard and Akira Hagiwara. And finally, I must thank my wife, Michiko Okazaki Sackett, not only for minding the home front while I was so often not around but also for her valuable assistance throughout.

There have been changes in the sumo world even in the brief time that has elapsed between taking the photographs and publication. (The promotions of Kitao and Hoshi mentioned above are good examples, as are the retirement of Aobajo and the departure of John Tenta from sumo.) There will be more. These photographs, and the text and captions, too, are offered as a documentary of the year I spent with sumo, which, though unforgettable, is past; I hope I have also captured the spirit of the sport and the rikishi, which is unchanging.

JOEL SACKETT

The *banzuke,* or list of rankings, for the Osaka tournament of 1985, when photography for *Rikishi* began.

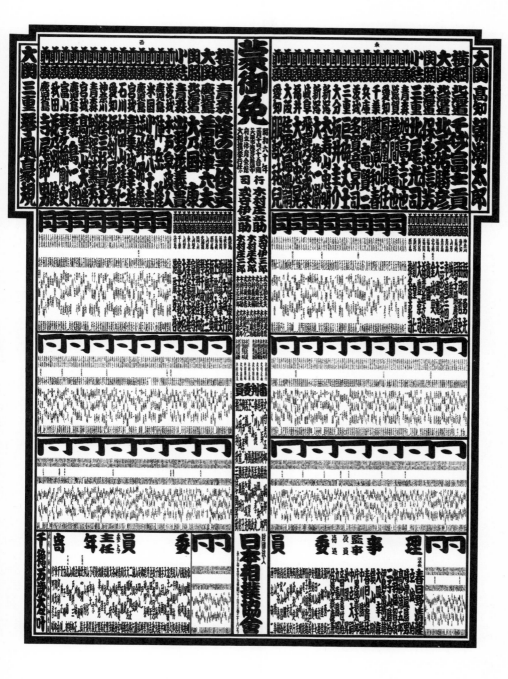

RIKISHI

Elaborate *kesho mawashi* (decorative aprons) contribute color to the *makuuchi* ring-entering ceremony, which takes place each day of a tournament before the makuuchi matches begin. Kesho mawashi are donated to a rikishi by sponsors, and have cost up to $900,000—though they are usually much less expensive.

Aobajo returns the dipper of *chikara mizu* (strength water) he rinses his mouth with to one of the announcers (*yobidashi*) before his bout begins.

A rikishi tosses salt into the ring before a match.

Hoshi uses the *nodowa* technique on his opponent, Kirinji, as the referee and judges look on.

The referee indicates the winning rikishi by pointing to his side, East or West, with the *gumbai* (war fan) he wields.

(*above and facing page*) Scenes from an early morning keiko session.

Temples usually serve as lodgings during regional tournaments.

An impromptu curbside gathering of yukata-clad rikishi.

Airing the keiko mawashi of a sekitori wrest

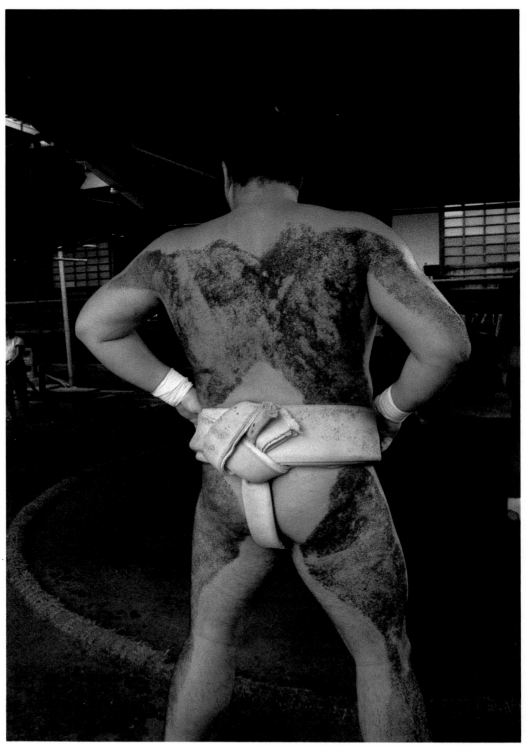

The telltale sign of defeat in the ring.

The Men of Sumo

First Encounter

It was over twenty-eight years ago—March 12, 1958, to be exact—that I first saw a sumo match and got close to the giant men of the sport. I had just arrived in Japan on January 10 of that year, which was also my twentieth birthday, and was living in Kobe with a Japanese family. They took me to Osaka to see the sumo tournament, or *basho,* and I was fascinated. Whatever my impressions were of those athletes in their scanty costumes performing exotic rites and routines, I certainly never dreamed that someday I would count them among my best friends.

There was no television where I lived, so I did not get to see sumo again until the *rikishi* (sumo wrestlers)[1] returned to Osaka the following year. I went three times to the basho, and then I moved to Tokyo, the home base of the sumo world today. I used to ride the train to Asakusabashi Station and walk the narrow streets watching the rikishi at work and play. I grew used to the distinctive smell of their hair wax and to their enormous size. I felt comfortable around them, but I did not have the courage to speak to them. What would they think of me? Probably I would be just another nuisance, a funny foreigner bothering them.

One day I was still in the area about 6:30 at night. I went into a small Japanese restaurant, the sort called a *snakku* ("snack") by the Japanese, and sat drinking sake and eating *yakitori* grilled over charcoal. Suddenly I smelled the distinctive odor of hair wax and knew that some rikishi had entered the restaurant. I turned and saw the famous *yokozuna* (grand champion) Asashio standing in the doorway dressed in a dark blue kimono. The people in the snack had all stopped eating and drinking;

---

[1] English sumo terminology isn't standardized, and often accurate, succinct translations cannot be found for Japanese terms, which I have chosen to use in their original form in many cases. For their precise definitions, the reader is referred to the Glossary of Sumo Terms.

some stood up, and a few even applauded—he was a real hero, and there I sat frozen with excitement. The yokozuna stopped and looked at me sitting at the counter, then walked on to his table with two elderly men—probably his sponsors.

I tried not to turn and stare too much at him, because he was seated facing my back. Two young rikishi, less well dressed, stood by the door ready to do whatever the great man asked. These were his *tsukebito*—rikishi who served as his personal attendants. (It is the privilege of all *sekitori,* or senior rikishi, to have tsukebito.) Everyone grew hushed, still talking but less loudly than before he had entered the room. He was watching me, and without any warning he stood up. The room was quiet as he walked up to me. *"Sake suki desu ka?"* (Do you like sake?) I was dumbfounded, almost speechless, but I managed to nod and say, *"Hai, suki desu."* (Yes, I do.)

He leaned forward and picked up my sake bottle from the counter and held it to pour for me. I needed both hands to steady the little sake cup, but I held it up, saying "Thank you." He poured and motioned for me to drink. I did, spilling part of it. He laughed, took the cup from my hand, and waited for me to pour for him. I did. He drank and returned to his table after patting me on the back, saying *"Gambatte"* ("good luck" or "keep trying").

An hour or so passed (it seemed like minutes to me), and I was getting a bit high on that delightful warm liquid. I stood up and walked over to the yokozuna's table with a full sake bottle. He smiled at me and held up his cup. I filled it. He drank and did the same for me. I drank less nervously than before and then repeated the process for each of the two old men with him. The yokozuna said something quite loudly, and the two young rikishi came rushing toward us. "Oh, God, I've done it now!" I thought, but they brought a chair for me and my dishes from the counter. *"Suwatte"* (sit down), he told me. Naturally I did, and then started one of the most amazing drinking bouts I have ever had.

Three or four hours later I was carried to the street by the two young rikishi, who hailed a taxi and put me in it. Asashio-*zeki* leaned in and asked if I had any money and where I was going. I told him I lived in Takadanobaba (very far from where we were) and that I had to take a train because a taxi was too expensive. He laughed and gave the driver a thousand yen (a lot of money then; my monthly gross income was only ¥90,000, which had to cover all my living expenses, including taxes!) and told me to visit his *heya* (headquarters) sometime.

The taxi rushed off into the night, and I looked back. He was there at the curb laughing and waving at me. I didn't know whether to feel foolish or happy and warm inside. In the end I did neither: I got sick.

It took a week to get over the hangover and a month to get up the courage to actually go to the heya to see Asashio-zeki again. When I finally went, it was a cold morning in January, and the tournament was on in Tokyo. I stood outside the doors to the heya for an hour. Young rikishi in their *mawashi* (wrestling belts) rushed in and out, not paying any attention to me. Then one of them recognized me and immediately went back inside. He soon returned and took my arm and led me inside. There was a mound of shoes in the entrance way; I added mine to the pile and found myself standing on wet sand in stocking feet.

The yokozuna was there and motioned for me to sit on a little platform area with some other people who were obviously visitors as well. There were about twenty rikishi practicing. I watched with amazement. Never had I been so close to sumo before. After about thirty minutes I lifted my intent gaze from the practice matches in progress and started looking around the huge room. Off to one side was a kitchen area where young rikishi were busy chopping vegetables and meat and tossing them into huge pots. There was a *tokoyama* (sumo hairdresser) kneeling on a small tatami area near the kitchen pulling the long hair of a rikishi and waxing it. As I observed the complicated process, fascinated, the distinctive sumo

topknot—the *chommage*—took shape. Other rikishi were helping each other put on their large *yukata* (casual cotton kimono) and bowing to each other, saying things I couldn't understand.

Was this really happening to me? Was I truly experiencing the inside world of sumo, the great traditional sport of Japan? After practice I was led to a *zabuton* (cushion) on another platform area and the yokozuna came in steaming from the bath. He sat down next to me, and in a moment we were both dipping into the boiling *chanko nabe* (a type of stew especially made for rikishi) in front of us. All the other rikishi stood as if at attention, waiting for his demands and comments. He ate quickly and left me. Immediately the younger rikishi sat down to eat, in order of their ranking. The pecking order of the sumo world was never more evident to me than at that moment, my first encounter with it.

Ever since the day I accepted Asashio-zeki's invitation to his heya, I have been involved in the lives of rikishi. Over the years, I have learned much about the tradition that governs their every move in public and even in the private of their homes, and I have come to be deeply impressed with the strength and persistence of that tradition among rikishi. To me, the most suggestive and striking symbol of that tradition is the chommage.

Famous people from the worlds of modern sports, entertainment, and politics, no matter how hotly pursued by their fans and the press, can get away, can put on sunglasses or change clothes and move about as they please; but the rikishi's chommage cannot be removed, and an active rikishi never knows the private pleasures of passing incognito. He is, by his very presence, always before the public eye, and consequently he must always behave as tradition dictates. Some successful rikishi actually become national heroes, and yet as long as they wear the chommage they remain bound to the traditions of their sport, restrictions that other ''superstars'' would never accept. Once the chommage is ceremonially cut off and they retire, they regain some degree of privacy, though they

are by no means free of the traditional duties and obligations of the sumo world.

Though today the hairstyle of the rikishi is one of his most outstanding physical characteristics, it was not always so, for the chommage was once the nearly universal fashion of the Japanese male—though it varied in as many ways as men's hairstyles do today. The topknot went out of favor among the populace during the Meiji period (1868–1912), when Western clothes came into vogue, but the sumo world decided to keep it as its symbol.

The chommage is so important to rikishi that one of the few forbidden methods of attacking your opponent is by pulling his hair. Before or after a bout, fans often reach out to touch the rikishi, and this is accepted as the tribute it is, a means of sharing in the power of these preeminent symbols of strength. Touching almost anywhere is permitted—except, once again, on the head. Anyone who forgets that unspoken rule is likely to be shocked at the response he receives from the rikishi or the tsukebito attending him!

In the latter part of the Edo period (approximately 150 years ago) the chommage was formed by shaving the front part of the head, creating what appeared to be a very high forehead indeed, with the long hair pulled back tightly and then folded forward in some form of a topknot. The hair was heavily oiled, frequently with camellia oil, to keep it in place. Although the Japanese have always been frequent bathers, they did not wash their hair very often. It took a professional to put a person's hair back in the special style—often indicating age, rank, or even profession—that he or she wore.

Today, the forelocks are no longer cut. The rikishi's head is shaved in the center, and the hair is pulled back and folded forward. A sweet-smelling pomade is used, making the hair stiff so that it holds its shape even during wrestling. The professional chommage stylist no longer exists

on street corners, and the sumo tokoyama came into being toward the beginning of the Meiji period to keep the sumo rikishi's hair in good condition and appearance. Some of these highly skilled men are the fourth or fifth generation of their families to be in the profession. In accord with the hierarchy of the sumo world, young apprentice tokoyama can only arrange the hair of young rikishi; two years of work under the supervision of a senior are required before the tokoyama can dress the hair of a senior rikishi. Incidentally, an entire bottle of shampoo is needed to wash a rikishi's hair and get the wax and sand out.

Hairstyle is far from the only aspect of the sumo rikishi's life that is strictly circumscribed by tradition and regulated by the Sumo Kyokai, the professional association composed of retired rikishi that governs the sport. In public, the rikishi must always wear either kimono or yukata, and for formal occasions they are compelled to wear traditional formal wear: kimono, *haori* (a kimono jacket), and the culotte-like garment called *hakama.* There are exceptions to these rules, and one of the most notable is that rikishi can wear Western clothes when they play baseball or golf, two of their favorite pastimes. Lounging around the heya, which is where all the unmarried rikishi live, they frequently wear jogging outfits that are specially made for them. There is no heat in a sumo heya, and a warm outfit feels good in the winter.

In the clothes and hairstyle of another age, the young rikishi are conspicuous in public. The occasional night off and trip to a disco is hard for them, but young rikishi can be seen, especially at Roppongi in Tokyo, dancing away in their kimono and chommage. The elders of the Sumo Kyokai frown on this, but they realize that unless they permit the youngsters to participate in some modern activities, the sumo world will never be able to recruit the people it needs.

Eating is restricted and controlled as well. The famous chanko nabe that is eaten by all rikishi is delicious. It can be made with anything from

fish to meat to poultry and generally includes a large quantity of fresh vegetables, too. Of course many large bowls of plain white rice are consumed with this stew. But chanko nabe is not all the rikishi eat. Contrary to uninformed popular opinion, they partake of a varied and balanced diet: there are usually large platters of various kinds of fish (cooked and uncooked), salads, and even giant steaks (at least for the senior rikishi) on the table. Snacks are permitted but not encouraged. Since the young rikishi have no cash to speak of, they frequent the inexpensive and filling noodle shops that are the regular haunts of students and workers—and of course MacDonald's hamburgers are not overlooked by these ''growing boys,'' either.

The kitchen of each heya is usually in the charge of one of the rikishi who has been there for a long time but has not progressed to a particularly high rank. It is not an unusual sight to see the heya chef dressed in yukata and astride a bicycle on his way to the local shops to select additional vegetables, fish, and meat, plus some beer or whisky—for the sekitori are permitted to drink alcohol with their meals.

The list of dos and don'ts of the sumo world is a long one. The world outside the closed sumo community is seldom aware of all the demands and restrictions with which the rikishi must contend and under which they must live, but these are what have been responsible for keeping sumo in the tradition of the past, and that in turn is what so many outside of sumo find appealing today. Young rikishi frequently balk at many of the demands made on them; they spend their early years as servants, running errands for the sekitori and the heya. But the *oyakata* (retired rikishi acting as coaches) and senior rikishi, who have had long experience in the sport, realize the importance of maintaining tradition and force them to follow the straight and narrow path of the sumo world.

To people who don't know the rikishi, their cherubic faces often seem incongruous with their formidable size and strength. In truth, most rikishi

are mild-mannered, kind men. They grow up together in their heya with respect and concern for each other. They develop a tremendous love for children and are extremely kind and patient with them. They are also professional sportsmen and recognize the importance of their fans and spend a great deal of time with them. Almost all eventually get married and have families, and their devotion to their wives and children is remarkable among Japanese men. They are hardworking and totally absorbed in their sport, so that most have few outside friends.

A rikishi is considered one of the finest catches a young girl can make. Many outsiders are surprised when a sumo rikishi marries a fashion model or well-known entertainer. This is not peculiar in the world of sumo. Stop and think about it: if successful, the rikishi is wealthy; in any event, he is a loving and caring family man and the epitome of Japanese manliness—a combination hard for Japanese women to pass up.

BACKGROUND

The tradition of the chommage is something that very few people, even among the Japanese, know much about or really understand, for it is a special world unto itself. The origins of sumo are buried in myth and early historical writings, but there is little doubt that some form of wrestling with its origin in India came to Japan from China twelve hundred to fifteen hundred years ago. The sport as we know it now developed slowly over the centuries, and whatever its origins, it is distinctly and exclusively Japanese today. The archives of the new Kokugikan sumo stadium at Ryogoku are filled with fascinating writings and artwork dating back to the ninth century. Descriptions of a ritual wrestling bout in which two large, muscular men are pitted against each other can also be found in

Japanese literature and art from the seventh century, according to Kasugano oyakata, the head of the Sumo Kyokai.

It is reported that early sumo matches were a form of religious ceremony or ritual dedicated to the gods with prayers for a bountiful harvest. Sumo was often performed along with ritual dancing and religious dramas. The Sumo Kyokai pamphlet on the sport says that as early as the Nara period (646–794) sumo was introduced into the ceremonies of the imperial court. For the next twelve hundred years it was closely associated with the aristocracy, and the emperor and other members of the imperial family still attend sumo tournaments regularly, as do visiting dignitaries.

Most of the ritual that precedes sumo matches today stems from the days when sumo was conducted at Shinto shrines. The roof hanging over the eighteen-foot-square, two-foot-high ring (*dohyo*) is reminiscent of a Shinto shrine. The straw rope that encircles the ring, fifteen feet in diameter, is representative of the straw bales of rice presented to the shrines.

The rules of sumo are simple: to win you simply force your opponent out of the ring or cause any part of his body other than the bottom of his feet—even his hair!—to touch the ground, either inside or outside the ring. The Sumo Kyokai lists the few taboos of sumo as follows: no closed fists, hair pulling, eye gouging, choking, or kicking in the stomach or chest—not that many rikishi could kick as high as his opponent's stomach or chest. It is also prohibited to seize the part of your opponent's belt covering the vital organs. Otherwise anything goes, and rikishi aren't matched according to weight or size as in Western boxing.

The throwing of salt and rinsing of the mouth with water before a bout are also part of the ritual dating back to the Shinto-related origins of the sport in Japan. Even the white rope wrapped around and tied at the yoko-zuna's waist, which he wears for the pre-bout ritual called the ring-enter-

ing ceremony (*dohyo iri*) has its origin in the Shinto *shimenawa* rope.

Sumo was always a professional sport; the rikishi were housed, fed, clothed, and paid by their feudal lords in the past, as they are by the Sumo Kyokai today. Aspiring young rikishi performed the duties of servants and studied and practiced under the tutelage of their seniors—a system that continues today.

There was a time when it was feared that sumo would die out. With the collapse of the feudal system that supported sumo in the Meiji era, sumo almost ceased to exist. Small professional groups banded together, however, and a rivalry between Osaka and Tokyo sumo groups developed. Finally the sport as we know it today evolved, and the Sumo Kyokai grew into its present form.

The formal organization of the sumo heya and the rankings of rikishi are fascinating subjects, but a detailed discussion of them is out of place in the present work. There are a number of excellent books in several languages available on the sport of sumo and its history, and to them I direct the reader for a full presentation of those aspects of sumo. I wish to focus instead on what I know best and have seen the most of over the years: the rikishi, the men of sumo, their daily lives, pastimes, training, and traditions. The best way to explain these things, I believe, is to follow a rikishi through the long hours of a hypothetical day, from morning to evening. In this way, I hope to give you a taste of the life of the great athletes of sumo.

MORNING

Much of the year, morning at a sumo heya begins long before the sun rises. The young rikishi sleep together in large rooms; each has his in-

dividual futon mattress, a quilt, and one box of possessions. They awake while it's still dark to face a long, hard day of work, practice, and study. They put on their mawashi (the six- to eight-meter-long sumo belt that they wrap around themselves something like a loincloth), tug at their chommage to straighten it as best they can, and put their futon away. The extreme cold in the rooms in the winter encourages them to get moving.

The dormitory-style toilets are all flushing, young men are standing around splashing cold water on their faces and brushing their teeth. By 5:30 or 6:00 A.M. they are downstairs warming up by exercising in the practice area, which is made of hard, pounded clay covered with a thin layer of damp sand. There is an official-size sumo dohyo for practice. The names of all the rikishi are written on wooden plaques that hang on the wall in order of their ranking. A small Shinto shrine is at one end of the room; all rikishi clap their hands and reverently bow to the shrine as they start their day.

No one is permitted to eat or drink anything before practice—they might get sick when hit in the stomach or need to use the toilet, which entails removing the long mawashi, and there is no time for such personal attention.

Some sweep the sand and remove any lumps or bits of trash, while others are getting food out of the refrigerator for later preparation. By 7:00 or 7:30 one or more of the oyakata arrive and take their places to supervise the practice. They leave their shoes at the entrance, and one of the youngsters quickly sets to polishing them. The oyakata are offered hot tea, and formal practice begins.

''Bang!'' goes the long bamboo stick of the oyakata against one of the bare rear ends, accompanied by a shouted instruction as to how to improve sumo technique. About 8:00 or 8:30 the door opens and the sekitori start to arrive, either from their own homes or their private rooms upstairs.

Young rikishi rush to the arriving seniors and help them remove their kimono and put on their mawashi, while others head to the rooms of the senior rikishi upstairs or offer them water to rinse out their mouths (but not to swallow) with long-handled bamboo cups. *Keiko* (practice matches) continues with the more senior youngsters pitted against each other. The sekitori, who join in the shouting of advice, instruction, and insults about mistakes, start doing warming-up exercises on the sides, assisted by their tsukebito. Finally the time arrives for the sekitori to practice. They select their grappling partners as the tsukebito ceremoniously wipe them off with towels and stand ready to provide any service required. If a junior should beat a sekitori, he is immediately challenged again until the sekitori wins. If lower-ranking rikishi don't step forward enthusiastically for a chance to practice with the sekitori, the bamboo stick is quickly felt against their bare skin, leaving a bright red sting.

In the meantime those who are on kitchen detail have started chopping, boiling, and preparing the meal that will follow practice at around 11:00 A.M. The acting ''head chef'' has gone off to shop, and others are upstairs cleaning the rooms and toilets. Two young rikishi are busy preparing the large *furo* (Japanese bath) with steaming hot water and making sure that all is immaculate.

There is so much early morning activity in a heya that the visitor is unable to take it all in at once, and he is not encouraged to do so: it is considered impossibly rude to place your back toward the ring, where the practice is taking place. Now the tokoyama has arrived and is cleaning his combs and wetting the small cloths he uses in dressing the rikishi's hair. He also spends a good deal of time rolling the paper string that is used to tie the hair at strategic points to maintain the chommage.

Youngsters help each other tighten their mawashi or brush sand out of their chommage. Once in a while the string comes loose during the strenuous practice, and another youngster will quickly step forward to

help retie it temporarily. Though a strict pecking order is rigorously maintained, there is always, at the same time, concern for one's fellows. *"Thud"* on the sand goes the loser, and *"bang"* goes the bamboo stick. It's a rough way to start the day.

The end of practice is marked by a pushing exercise: one rikishi braces himself in the center of the ring and another charges him with all his might, pushing him backward to the edge of the ring. Then the charger's head is pushed down until he finally falls, never putting out his hand or arms to brace his crashing to the hard clay and sand floor. It is important to be able to fall without reaching out. After all, whoever touches the ground with any part of the body or steps outside the ring first loses the match.

The dohyo has been swept several times during keiko to keep it clean. Water is sprinkled on the sand, and the senior rikishi throw salt to purify the area before they practice. No one ever walks there in shoes; it would be a sacrilege to do so.

At last practice is over and the rikishi line up neatly and do a strenuous series of calisthenics, helping each other with the more difficult ones, such as sit-ups and touching the head to the ground while seated in a spread-eagle position. After the last exercise they squat on the balls of their feet, close their eyes, and meditate—mental concentration is one of the most important components of sumo technique. To mark the end of morning training, they clap their hands and bow to the shrine.

Strange as it might seem, even this morning session is not a private affair of the heya. It has been closely observed by sports writers and other journalists. Frequently television crews and radio interviewers stand around catching side comments and filming the rikishi. Nothing goes unnoticed, as fans wander in and out all the time.

Some of the most frequent visitors from outside the sumo world are the neighbors. Just think what it must be like to have thirty or more hefty

rikishi move in next door, with the inevitable commotion, their unique routine, and their exotic presence! The oyakata and rikishi are well aware of the inconvenience they may cause to their neighbors and make every effort to compensate for it; in fact, they go so far that they may be some of the best neighbors one could hope to have. The children who live nearby are all known to the heya by name and are allowed in to watch practice and share meals most of the time. The housewife who runs out of eggs after the shops have closed knows perfectly well she can find anything she needs in her sumo neighbor's pantry and that she is welcome to it. Fathers and sons often join in games of catch with the young rikishi. In most cases, the neighborhood around a heya runs much like a happy extended family. This same atmosphere is created when the rikishi travel outside Tokyo to temporary sites for a provincial tournament or to exhibition bouts in the countryside.

The nearby shops have little reason to complain about a heya in their midst, since their sumo neighbors have voracious appetites and consume a great deal of almost everything. The many visitors to the heya also buy flowers, beverages, and other tokens and gifts, supporting a legion of small shop owners. Hundreds of sumo-related meetings are conducted over endless cups of coffee at the nearest coffee shop. To be a good neighbor, the wife of an oyakata may even fill in as free extra help when one of the shopkeepers in her neighborhood is ill or overly busy.

After a relaxing hot bath, during which the sekitori are scrubbed down by their tsukebito, the first meal of the day is ready. Naturally the bathing is done in order of rank, and the most junior rikishi won't have a chance to bathe until lunch is over and the kitchen cleaned up.

Several years ago there was a famous incident, when a photographer broke a window above the bath trying to get his camera through a narrow space to photograph a yokozuna in the tub. The glass came shattering down over the nude yokozuna sitting in the hot water; needless to say, the

photographer had to be assigned to a different beat by his company for his own protection.

Eating is generally done rather quickly—again in order of rank. The sekitori may ask one or two visitors whom he knows to join him, and together they drink a small amount of beer as they start to eat. The food is delicious, but guests are asked not to take too long, as all the other rikishi are waiting for the space around the boiling pot for their chance to eat. The poor lowest-ranked rikishi get the bottom of the pot (mainly broth) and cold rice and pickles. Theirs is a hard life—a tepid, cold, murky bath; leftover rice and the dregs of the stew; and no beer, either, for he's got a long day ahead.

The laundry must be done and the kimono of the sekitori, as well as shirts and trousers of the oyakata, must be ironed. The heya has to be cleaned, too, and some young rikishi have to go off to the school run by the Sumo Kyokai for lessons in calligraphy, sumo history, or other subjects, while others go to the bank or shopping for the heya. As always, people are watching them.

The sekitori have their own duties as well. Fans and sponsors send large blank cards to the heya with a cash donation. What they seek are *tegata,* or hand prints. The sekitori make these by banging their palms onto huge red or black ink pads and then stamping their hands on the cards one by one. They are usually assisted, in an assembly-line fashion, by two or more tsukebito—the blank cards are stacked in front of the sekitori and one tsukebito removes the stamped card and places it aside to dry while the other tsukebito restack them. Then each card must be signed by the sekitori with ink and brush. When the cards are finished they are returned to the individual who brought them and are used as personal mementos or, more frequently, as corporate gifts. Sometimes a rikishi will make up to one thousand tegata in one sitting; this is tiring work for all concerned, but especially for the sekitori.

In 1985, for example, yokozuna Chiyonofuji made more than twenty-seven thousand tegata. He and his tsukebito also estimate that he signed his name over fifteen thousand additional times on everything from pieces of paper, photos, and sumo programs to handkerchiefs, shirts, and even panties!

The tegata hand-imprinting and signing process takes hours, and in boredom the mischievous sekitori frequently draw cartoon glasses, moustaches, and huge lips on the tsukebito assisting them with the brush and black ink. This harmless fun—the ink washes off easily—gives everyone a laugh and breaks the tension and tedium of the task.

The morning is coming to an end. For the leading sekitori, it may be wrapped up with an interview or two or a meeting with the heya's oyakata about the schedule for the next couple of weeks. This rigorous schedule is observed daily except for five days after each of the six annual tournaments. Even during that holiday period, the cleaning, cooking, and general housework must be done by the young rikishi. The schedule is maintained as well during the long and tiring countryside tours called *jungyo,* the only difference being that it takes place in a different city or town almost every day. Whether at home base or on the road, the morning of the sekitori concludes with a short nap. For the lower-ranked rikishi, that luxury remains a dreamed-of future privilege to which he aspires.

Afternoon

After the hectic morning, one might think that the sumo world would take a little rest, but that is far from the case. If the morning is devoted to training and practice, the afternoon is given to a variety of public relations and promotional activities, which frequently bring in extra cash as well. Younger rikishi either remain in the heya finishing their chores, or they attend the sumo school. The task of representing sumo to the world at large falls to the sekitori, whose tsukebito are busy running errands for them and getting them dressed in preparation for the round of activities that make up the afternoon schedule.

If a tournament is in progress, the tokoyama is harassed with requests from everyone to have their chommage fixed, and young rikishi are running off to the stadium for their bouts. The sekitori depart for the long sit in the *shitaku beya* (dressing room) awaiting the time for the dohyo iri, which takes place before the series of bouts of the higher-ranked rikishi. They patiently stare into space; the interval serves as a "psyching up" period during which they clear their minds and concentrate on the all-important few minutes—or more likely, seconds—they are going to have on the tournament dohyo in front of the public and the television cameras. The activity around them doesn't seem to bother them, but, significantly, no one in the room talks.

At tournament time, the sekitori and the heya frequently send small presents or the tournament *banzuke*—the list of the current rankings written in old-style Japanese characters—to their friends and fans. These must all be hand addressed with ink and brush in artistic Chinese characters, and it is the job of the young rikishi to help with this. Thousands of envelopes and packages must be addressed, stuffed, and posted.

If there is no tournament, the afternoon schedule is different, though no less hectic. Most of the sekitori rush off to make public appearances for charities, standing on street corners to launch the Red Feather (Community Chest) drive or stationing themselves at department stores, temples, or shrines to encourage people to donate to some worthy cause. The sekitori digs deeply into his own purse to donate to charities for hand-

icapped persons and the elderly, and for such commendable projects as new sports and education facilities for the underprivileged.

The police and fire departments also depend on these famous men to help publicize their public service campaigns. The senior rikishi are so popular that these authorities are convinced their safety programs are much more effective if the rikishi make appearances to assist them. Many of the rikishi make public appearances to encourage people to be more careful with fire, avoid drugs, drive carefully, and be sure to lock their doors at night. The fire department regularly features rikishi on posters, a tradition that goes back to the Edo period, when rikishi were sometimes called upon to help the flamboyant fire squads of old Tokyo in the constant battle against "the flowers of Edo."

School visits, which are considered great fun by all in the sumo world, are another part of their afternoon activities. Rikishi travel to schools all around the country and talk with the children about trying harder in school and listening to their parents. There are moments of general play with the students, and visits often end in a great free-for-all, with the little ones yelling and laughing as they attack the huge, kimono-clad rikishi en masse. Everyone has a good time, and the goodwill generated for the future of the sport is enormous.

The rikishi's busy afternoon agenda continues. Though much of what he does is volunteer work to build goodwill, some of it is also profitable. Even so, the obligation of the chommage far outweighs the drive for monetary gain in most individuals. They feel a heavy moral obligation to the public and their position and are very serious and sincere in their efforts to fulfill these obligations. In the afternoon, *koen kai* (fan club) sponsors and heya sponsors, usually business executives, must be visited in their offices, and talks about future plans for the heya are conducted over endless cups of tea. The visiting rikishi shake the hands of the customers and the company staff, giving the businessman and his firm great "face."

These visits, while necessary for the popularity of the individual rikishi and his heya, also provide part of their income, as sponsors play an important part in sumo finance.

Sign *kai* (autograph sessions) are frequently conducted in the afternoon at department stores or at the openings of new restaurants, coffee shops, pachinko (a kind of pinball) parlors, and just about every other type of establishment. By either direct contact or through the oyakata, the owners have requested particular rikishi to make an appearance to promote their business. The forthcoming appearance is announced to customers through advertisements or direct mail and posters. At these sessions, again, the rikishi shake thousands of hands, sign autographs, and pose for endless photos with the customers—all in the course of a couple of hours.

On such occasions, the rikishi are given envelopes of cash, the amount varying according to the popularity and rank of the rikishi and the relationship between the business and the rikishi or his heya. The money is frequently shared with the heya, and a small amount is also given to each of the tsukebito who accompany the sekitori. If the event has been arranged by the Sumo Kyokai, the sekitori must share part of his money with the association. The amount of cash in these envelopes can sometimes be fairly large, but the actual amount that each participant ends up getting is not that big once it has been shared.

The ever-present fans frequently stuff small amounts of cash, either in envelopes with notes or simply in the form of folded bills, into the obi around the sekitori's kimono-clad waist. This is sometimes referred to as "mawashi money," and it is found and collected when the tsukebito undress the sekitori upon his return. The tsukebito untie the obi and the sekitori slowly turns and the obi is removed. The tsukebito collect the envelopes and cash as they fall to the tatami floor.

When talking about money, the sumo world generally uses the cardinal numbers one, two, three, and so on, to refer to one ¥10,000 note, two

¥10,000 notes, three ¥10,000 notes, and so forth. Amounts smaller than ¥10,000 are not generally given to rikishi unless they are quite young. Normally one should think in terms of three, five, seven, ten, and up.

As any businessman who has spent time in Japan well knows, it is a country of meetings and endless discussions. Sumo is no exception, and the afternoons are very often filled with meetings for all levels of the sumo world. The Sumo Kyokai elders (*toshiyori*) spend a great deal of time discussing rulings and ways of maintaining the sport and its tradition. Dealing with the ever-encroaching modernization of the lives of the rikishi and all the individuals involved in the sport is a problem for these older men. Finances must also be discussed, for it takes enormous sums of money to run the sumo world, and this flow of funds must be closely controlled and kept honest and proper.

Yakuza, the famous gangsters of Japan, are always trying to work their way into the sport. It normally has nothing to do with betting or attempts to fix a bout, as the press sometimes suggests. These men of the underworld also want the ''face'' of association with the famous personalities of sumo. The temptation to cooperate must be great for the rikishi and oyakata, but they make every effort to avoid any tainted association, otherwise the public would soon lose respect for their heroes and interest in the sport would wane.

The afternoon is not all work, for one must remember that these are very young men, frequently from rural Japan and generally with no more than a high-school education. They start when they are fifteen or sixteen years old in most cases, and at that age, they need to let loose from time to time. General horseplay behind the scenes is great fun to observe, but the public never has a chance. A quick stop at a pachinko parlor is a pleasant relief for many of the fellows, and *hanafuda* (a Japanese card game) may be played quickly in a quiet corner by several of the rikishi. Mah-jongg is immensely popular, and of course everyone has a Walkman tape recorder

and many have small television sets. Real gambling as such is not much practiced; the amounts bet on a card game or mah-jongg session are not unduly large, and it's more the fun of the break and the chance to win that is important. Outsiders are practically never included in any of this, which only involves companions from your own heya.

Most of the sumo world is musical, and the rikishi enjoy singing and playing the guitar or some other instrument. They practice for the time when they will have an opportunity to stop at a *karaoke* bar, where patrons sing popular songs to taped background music. On some occasions they are also expected to entertain guests: at the heya parties when fans come to celebrate the end of a tournament, or upon the visit of the sumo group to a regional city or town during their provincial touring.

The inevitable snack of a hamburger or hot dog, ice cream cone or bowls of *ramen* or *soba* also makes the afternoon much more tolerable. Still, they limit their intake of sweets on their own initiative, for there is a fear among all sumo rikishi of diabetes, one of the most common diseases among the participants of the sport.

They are sportsmen, and they enjoy other types of athletic competition as well. Since sumo depends on strict muscular control and top physical condition, rikishi also excel in other sports, with baseball and golf the most popular. A game of catch and batting practice with a rikishi is a dangerous pastime, however, for the outsider. The rikishi forget their own strength when pitching a ball to us, and one can end up with a very sore hand catching a ball thrown by a 180-kilogram wrestler. Bats for "alley baseball" may be anything from a real baseball bat to a bamboo pole or a broomstick. The ball is often made by rolling the adhesive tape from bandages into a tight, round glob. The sumo world has to be the largest customer in Japan for the bandage manufacturers, as minor injuries such as pulled muscles, cuts, bruises, and dislocated finger or toe joints are an everyday occurrence.

Golf is the game the majority of the rikishi aspire to play—most Japanese males feel the same way about the sport. Senior sumo rikishi and oyakata frequently become exceptional golfers, and many have single handicaps. Their main problem with this sport is finding the time to play. The tremendous control and athletic prowess of the sekitori is readily acknowledged by many professional Japanese sportsmen, and a mutual admiration society convenes when a famous pro golfer visits a golfing sekitori at his heya. Each asks the other for his autograph, and they lay enthusiastic plans for the day when they will have time to play a casual game together.

Baseball also has its avid fans in the sumo world. Kurama-zeki, one of the longtime popular sekitori, dreams of playing baseball for the Hanshin Tigers. He is such a fan of the popular team that he almost missed his bout at a basho because the Tigers were batting on television when his time to enter the ring arrived.

Fishing is enjoyed by many sumo rikishi and oyakata, and you have never seen a more contented human being than a rikishi with a fishing rod in one hand and a beer in the other. Since, in the process of their rise through the heya hierarchy, they all have had to learn how to cook, you can expect a downright spectacular meal when they get back after a successfull day fishing.

The setting sun does not mean the end of work for the men of sumo, but simply a change in routine. For as the afternoon comes to an end, the evening meal must be started and the sekitori's outfit—kimono, obi, *tabi* (Japanese-style socks with a separation for the big toe), wristwatch, and other possessions must be laid out and ready for him to have put on so he can fulfill his nighttime obligations.

EVENING

As night descends the sumo world changes its pace, but there is little rest. Visitors stop at the heya and are asked to join in the evening meal, which has been carefully prepared by the young rikishi. The oyakata sit in smaller rooms talking with former fans from their wrestling days, and the sekitori must make brief appearances to be photographed, sign autographs, and show an interest in the visitors. The usual endless series of questions ensues as to why things are done the way they are in sumo. Presents from the visitors are heaped upon the rikishi, and the envelopes of cash change hands again.

The time then comes for the nighttime prowl with fans and a few select friends. The sekitori are dressed, and sometimes one or two of the tsukebito are taken with them when they go to meet businessmen and their guests at restaurants and bars or clubs. They can relax a little more with these people than they could during the day, but it is still work.

The ability of the rikishi to consume alcohol is famous in Japan, but it is also sometimes overstated. It is true, however, that the average person who thinks he can keep up with the sekitori drinking generally cannot. One reason is that the sekitori all eat before they leave the heya to meet people. They are not drinking on an empty stomach like the person who has come directly from his office after a long day at work. Even taking that into account, though, there is no doubt that the ability of the sekitori to consume alcohol is exceptional. An entire bottle of whisky or cognac can be consumed over a period of a couple hours without any major effect on the wrestler, in telling contrast to their host and the other outsiders with them.

The rikishi feel a responsibility to avoid public drunkenness, even among friends. Getting drunk is taboo in the sumo world, for the rikishi must always preserve the image of the chommage in both his public and

private behavior. Perhaps there are practical reasons as well—who knows what damage a huge rikishi who has forgotten his strength might wreak in a tiny Japanese nightspot!

Patrons and sponsors are frequently guilty of insisting that the sekitori accompany them to public places where people will not leave them alone. In these cases, the tsukebito is forced to stand guard, nursing one drink and keeping a constant watch to prevent people from pestering the sekitori and mauling him in drunken admiration. Though the rikishi are experts at the endless nonsensical chatter that makes up much of the night life of Japan, many of these nights on the town, in spite of being planned with the best intentions by the host, turn out to be boring and irritating for the poor rikishi.

You seldom see sekitori walking down the streets at night. Their large size and their distinctive dress and appearance make them conspicuous targets for overenthusiastic (and often, inebriated) fans, who are always shouting to them and accosting them. The sekitori can neither brush them off (that would be rude) or escape—the confines of kimono and geta (wooden Japanese sandals) prevent them from walking very quickly. To avoid such scenes, the sekitori take cars or taxis even when they are traveling no more than a block or so in an entertainment district. Taxi drivers are always proud to have them in their cars and never complain about the short distance, as they would to the average person.

Bar and club owners are delighted to have them visit their establishments, and the bill for the stay might be enormous, but it generally is picked up by the people accompanying them and not the rikishi themselves. Hostesses vie behind the scenes for a chance to sit next to the sekitori; though they remain jovial on the surface, most of this is a chore for the sekitori.

While the sekitori are out being wined and dined, the young rikishi are clearing up after the evening meal and putting everything back in place.

Then they have some free time, but there's not much to do. Besides a walk in the neighborhood and a stop at a local restaurant for another bowl of noodles or possibly a last try at a pachinko parlor, there may be a telephone call home, or a quiet time in the bath, one of the few private places they can go day or night! The young rikishi have to be in the heya by nine o'clock or so, unless they are accompanying an oyakata or sekitori.

Once in their common room they share their experiences, their aches and pains, and their periodic gripes with each other. Now is the time when the box or drawer containing all the worldly possessions of the young wrestler is opened and the contents surveyed with affection. Photos and letters are reexamined and put carefully back in their place of honor. They help each other with the last chores of making the futon and settle back to listen to music, practice a musical instrument, play with a small word processor, watch television, or massage the aching back or leg of a fellow rikishi. At last there is time to read the newspapers—that is if the oyakata and sekitori, who read them in the morning, haven't torn them up or scribbled notes all over them. They also enjoy reading comic books and, once in a while, a popular novel.

No bar hostesses hold out a glass of whisky for them, but there is at least a hint of the female presence in their lives. Young girls frequently go and stand outside the sumo heya hoping that one or more of the young rikishi will come out. It is all quite innocent and fun for both. They talk and the girls bring them presents and love letters written with all the enthusiasm of a fifteen-year-old school girl with a crush on a contemporary hero. In the evening, in their room together, the fellows share their letters and dream about the day they will have the freedom to actually spend time with girls.

There is one very real woman in the life of the young rikishi—the *okami-san,* or wife of the oyakata, and she plays a major role, for she is the mother figure for the heya. Homesickness is very real, and not only for the

newly arrived youngsters. Okami-san spends hours listening, helping with bandages, and generally being a foster mother. The youngsters have faced a man's world all day, a day that is harder than most adults in the outside world can even imagine, and the night takes its toll in loneliness, exhaustion, and anxiety.

Okami-san must also reassure the many anxious mothers from distant parts of Japan who call to find out how their "little boy" is doing. She is also generally the one who has to tell the young rikishi when someone in their family is ill or has died. If a death comes during a basho, the rikishi cannot abandon their sumo obligations to attend the funeral, and this is a heartrending experience. Okami-san is there to help, in both dire and daily circumstances, as are all their fellow rikishi.

The comradeship among the young rikishi is marvelous to witness, for they play father, big brother, and best friend to each other. Their whole world revolves around the twenty to thirty men in their heya. They share moments of joy as well as grief and loneliness with each other. The relationship they share is not unlike that of young men in a private school dormitory and is equally mischievous and innocent.

As it grows late, they start to drift off to sleep—though they must always be ready to jump up if the phone rings or a sekitori returns and needs to be undressed and cared for. By eleven or twelve o'clock the heya is silent, and weary bodies are getting that much-needed rest so they will be prepared for the next day and a repeat of the routine.

The sekitori have returned to their rooms or, if they are married, to their wife and family in their own homes. The oyakata takes one last look through the accounts and schedules for his heya and thinks about the future. His wife fixes a last drink or cup of tea they can share together as they consider their sumo "family" and their problems. The oyakata and his wife feel their responsibilities strongly. Mothers have entrusted their sons to them, expecting that they will be raised to be strong, honest men

well-trained in a profession—a risky profession, one that could bring wealth and fame but that for most only brings hard work, low remuneration, and an uncertain future. How to do the best for each of these men?—that is the question that the oyakata and his wife face anew every night.

It is at night that the loneliness of the world of the chommage is most evident. Rikishi can't associate with their fellows from other heya or the scandalous weekly magazines who follow them everywhere day and night will write that they are fixing bouts, or that there is some type of underhanded dealing going on. People from outside the sumo world are kind to them, but most of the time it is because they want something in return. In the end, they have each other and no one else.

Big Decisions and Retirement

The initial decision to go into sumo is a major one for a young man only fifteen or sixteen years old. Of course his parents help him with the decision, but he has to be certain it is what he wants to do. After all, the natural impulse for most of us at that young age is to play and enjoy life; very few teenagers are keen on working hard every day, without a holiday for months on end. The decision to continue when the going gets rough and to try harder is equally difficult. The long, hard-working days roll into weeks, then months, and each year seems like the last in the sumo world. High hopes of doing better in a bashō and being promoted in rank coexist with the fear of injury, an injury that might ruin it all or, at the very least, put you in the hospital so that you automatically drop back down in rank while convalescing and have to start up the ladder again.

The biggest decision of all comes for different rikishi at different ages and in different ways, but it is the same: is it time to retire and do something else, or should I push on? Rikishi who simply don't reach the top ranks and never become a sekitori are faced with that decision when they are still very young—perhaps in their mid-twenties. That is the age when other people are finishing their university education and thinking about their future. The less-than-successful rikishi, however, is already completing one career and determining where to go next.

Sumo Kyokai officials, the oyakata of each heya, and the other rikishi are all sympathetic and willing to listen and help, but the final decision must be made by the individual. Even the lowest-ranked rikishi, once he has grown his chommage, commands attention and respect from the general public. When he cuts the chommage off and retires, he is suddenly just another young man without a job.

Sekitori who have been clever, planned for the future, and saved money may be able to purchase a *toshiyori kabu,* or share in the Sumo Kyokai, and become an oyakata once they retire. The Sumo Kyokai lists 107 shares, and each one has a name. The previous owner or his family sell the share to a sekitori who is eligible, and shares can even be "rented" temporarily until the share a sekitori has planned to buy is available. The accepted age of retirement for an oyakata is sixty-five, at which time he is expected to sell his share and make way for another. But for the sekitori, the age of retirement comes when he can no longer perform well under the pressures and demands of the sumo life.

Of the 107 oyakata, a few will have their own heya. The others will be trainers in another oyakata's heya, and all will have positions in the Sumo Kyokai and a voice in the future of the sport. Throughout modern history there have been a few exceptions to the rule of 107 oyakata. In 1986 there were 109, because the great yokozuna Taiho and Kitanoumi were granted special status as oyakata and allowed to keep their own names and start

their own heya. Their names, however, will exist only as long as they are active. As "single-generation oyakata," their special status and names will die with them, and again there will only be 107 official oyakata.

Retirement comes earliest for the rikishi who never make the top. They are urged to make a decision about their own future before they get too old to change careers successfully. Outside the protective cocoon of the sumo heya is the cold world, and they are going to have to make their own way in it. Businesses related to food are probably the most common areas of work they select. Many open restaurants. They have had vast experience in shopping, food preparation, and keeping a kitchen in order, plus serving meals. Operating butcher shops or fish shops are also popular second careers for these men. However, to open your own chanko nabe restaurant or other small business takes money. There is no pension or severance pay for the rikishi, so they have to depend on others to help them, or their own modest savings. Many retiring rikishi return to their home prefecture, where they are local heroes even if they didn't become famous sekitori. Others find work near the heya and develop a business from the fans and people related to the heya.

The ceremony for a retiring rikishi who has not reached a high rank is simple, with friends and members of the heya gathering to take their turn at cutting off the chommage, a few strands of hair at a time. The senior oyakata makes the final cut and this removes the symbol of the rikishi. His name is then taken down from the wall of the heya and erased from the listings of the Sumo Kyokai. All those attending bring envelopes of money to help him in his new life, while others provide the food and drink. It is something like a family gathering, and his fellow rikishi quietly and somberly file up to snip the hair and bow to their friend. They know that this is going to happen to them someday, whether in the spectacular ceremony held for the retirement of a successful sekitori or the quieter, more personal event that they are participating in now.

Retirement naturally means more than just a change in routine for the sekitori; as an oyakata, their income is dramatically reduced, and they frequently run supplemental businesses such as restaurants and tourist facilities. They must be businessmen, trainers, keepers of the tradition, big brothers, and fathers. It is an around-the-clock job, but they appear to enjoy it. They also seem to enjoy the freedom that comes with the removal of the chommage. They can expand the circle of their personal friends and do more in public without the restraints of the sport's tradition. Some overstep the bounds of good judgment with this new freedom, and the Sumo Kyokai is quick to remind them that the spirit of the chommage must still be maintained even if it no longer rests on their heads.

The big day comes for the senior rikishi during the week following a tournament in Tokyo. The ceremony is conducted in the main stadium (Kokugikan) before a full house of twelve thousand spectators. It's a day packed with activity, starting with speeches by dignitaries from the retiring rikishi's koen kai. Then he is seated on a chair in the center of the dohyo. A *gyoji* (referee) in colorful kimono stands by with a tray and pair of scissors. People from all professions and walks of life who have been part of the rikishi's life come up one at a time to snip a strand or two of hair. Sometimes up to four hundred people will cut, and each name as it is called out brings memories to the sekitori as he sits there. The rikishi always try to restrain their emotions in public, never smiling when winning a bout or frowning in anger when losing. But on this occasion the taboo is lifted: now he simply cries, as the chommage is slowly being snipped away.

The final cuts are made by his fellow sekitori and the senior oyakata, who removes the entire topknot. Fans cheer and call out the rikishi's name for the last time, for he will have a new name from that time on.

While the retiring wrestler goes to the dressing room to be groomed by a professional barber and dressed in a suit and tie, all his fellow sekitori perform exhibition bouts to entertain the crowd. Some sing and others do slapstick comedy matches until the new oyakata is prepared to appear in his new image and life before the shouting, cheering crowd. He asks for their continued support and bows to the audience.

Parties follow and often go on to the wee hours of the morning. The chommage is reverently placed in a box and put in a place of honor either in their home or the heya. It will always be cherished with great pride, and children, grandchildren and future daughters- and sons-in-law will be shown it and told many stories of the days when he was a sekitori.

Thus ends the tale of the chommage, but it is an unending tale, for new chommage are being grown and groomed on the heads of young aspiring rikishi, and the spirit of sumo, the spirit of the chommage, continues, perpetuating one of Japan's greatest and oldest traditions.

PHOTOGRAPHS

Heya Life

Heya means room or chamber, but in sumo it is much more—the home and headquarters, the workplace and world of the rikishi. Here he lives and works with his "family": the oyakata who are his trainers and managers; the senior oyakata's wife, who is his surrogate mother; and his fellows, who are his grappling partners, teachers and students, and lifelong friends.

The heya routine is a rigorous one, beginning early in the morning and continuing until the late hours of the night. It is communal life Japanese style, shaped by hierarchies of seniority and rank, strict and demanding but also nurturing and supportive. It asks for total commitment from the rikishi: he gives it, or doesn't last too long.

In return, heya life does more than train bodies. It molds character, disciplines the spirit, and preserves the rituals and traditions of the ancient sport, passing on the intangible human inheritance of the sumo world to new generations of rikishi and their fans.

2

3

8

9

10

11

2

13

14

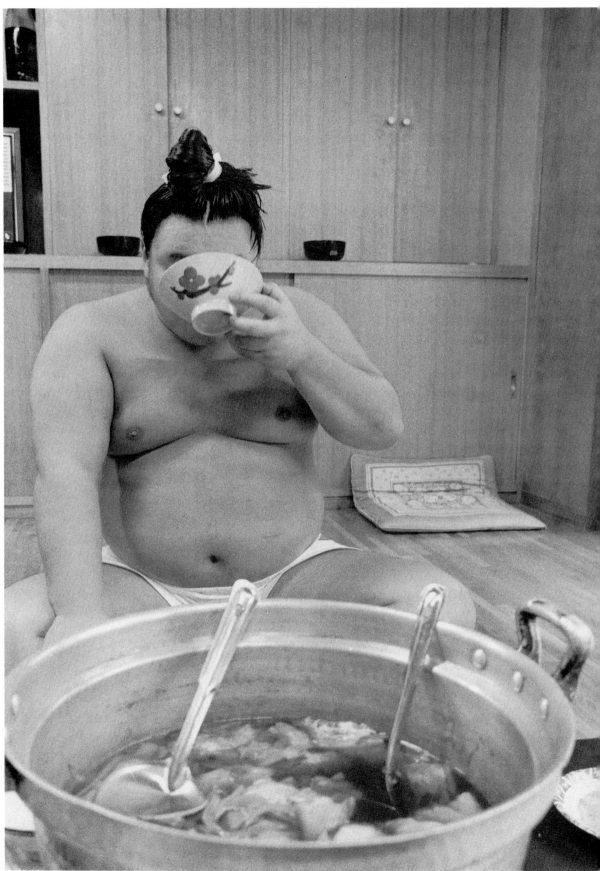

17

18

19

20

あぶないから
はいっては
いけません！

日本国土開発

日本国土開発

23

24

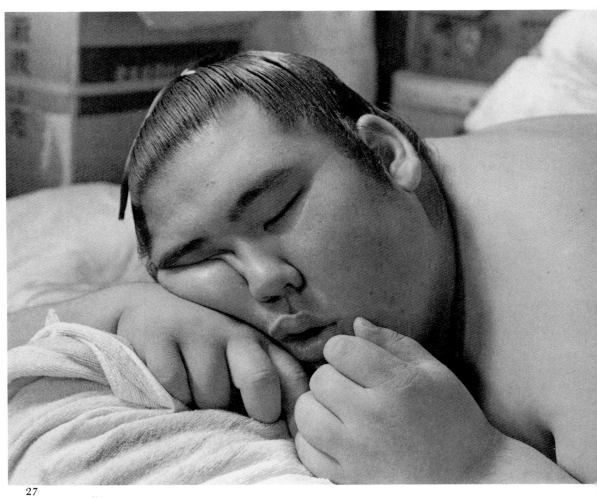

27

堂々とした態度で
一、言葉をはっきりと
一、思い切って
105

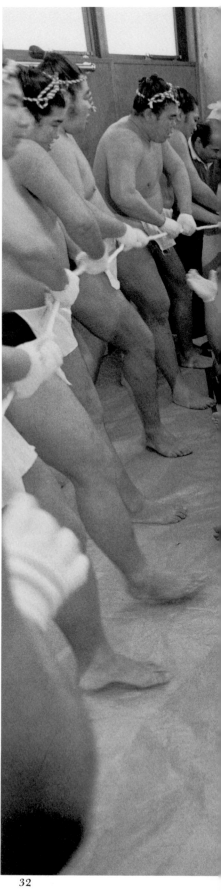

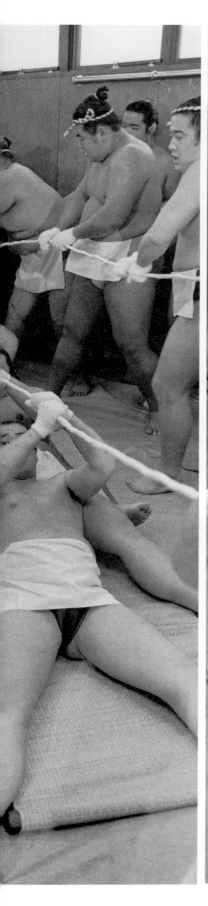

35

36

37

38

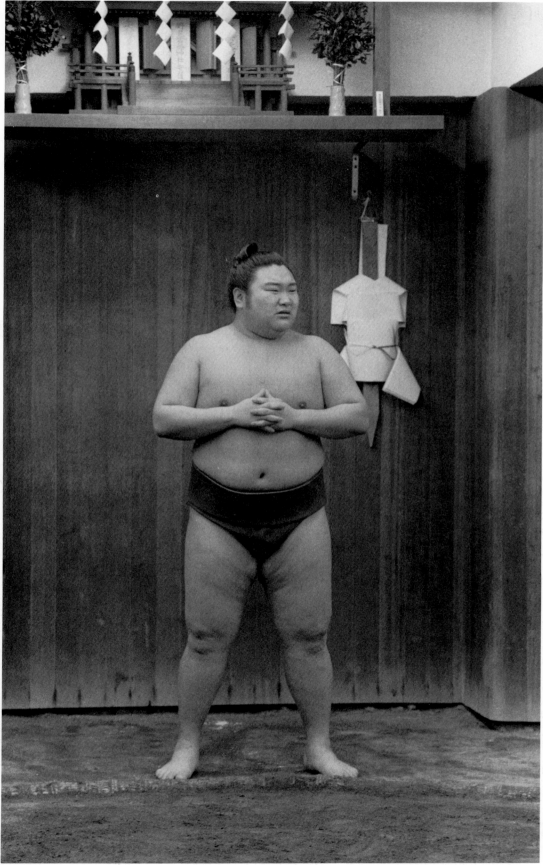

The Tournament

It is during the sumo tournament that the rikishi comes into his own. There his ranking, his salary, his success or failure in the sumo world are decided.

The hours before the rikishi is scheduled to appear in the ring are tense. He makes his way to the stadium—at the Kokugikan in Tokyo many fans wait at the entrance to watch their favorite rikishi arrive. He enters the shitaku beya, the dressing room, where he dresses and warms up for the bout; there he may practice his charge (tachiai) or a particular technique, or just sit and collect himself for those crucial moments in the ring when he faces his opponent of the day before a live audience of thousands and a television audience much, much larger.

The makuuchi bouts that are the highlight of the day's long program are preceded by the majestic makuuchi ring-entering ceremony, the parade of rikishi into the ring that gives the fans a chance to see all of the contestants who will compete. The day is capped by the yokozunas' bouts. But no matter what ranks of rikishi are competing, the resulting victory or defeat shapes their future in the sport.

43

44

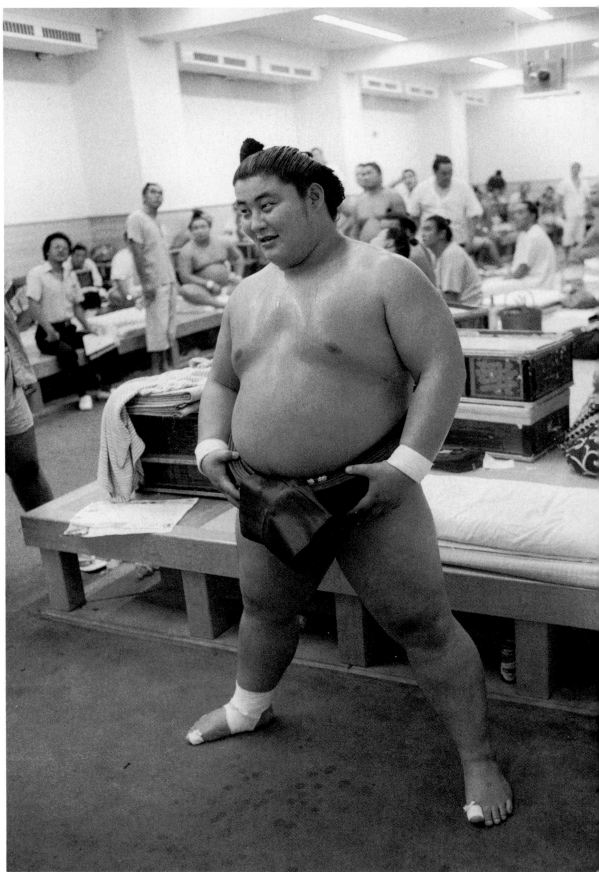

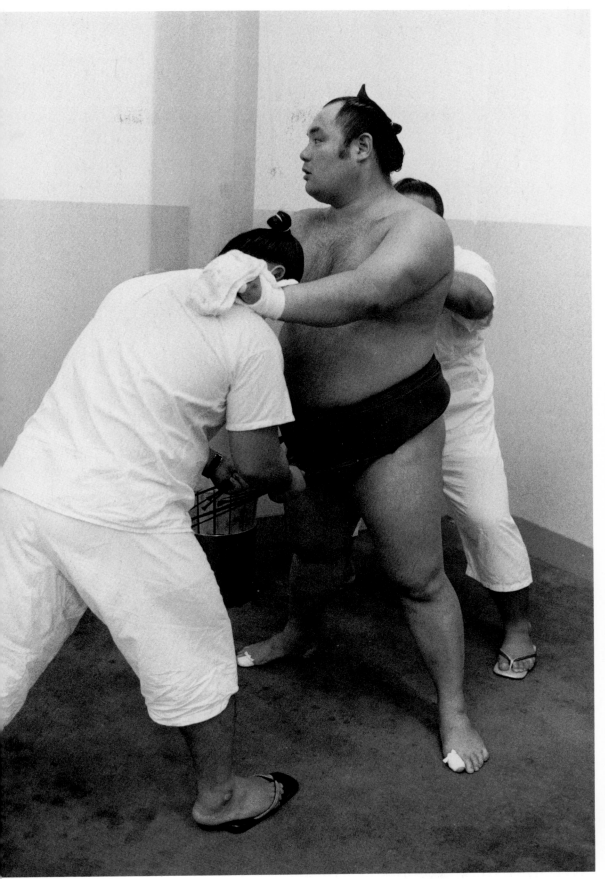

48

49

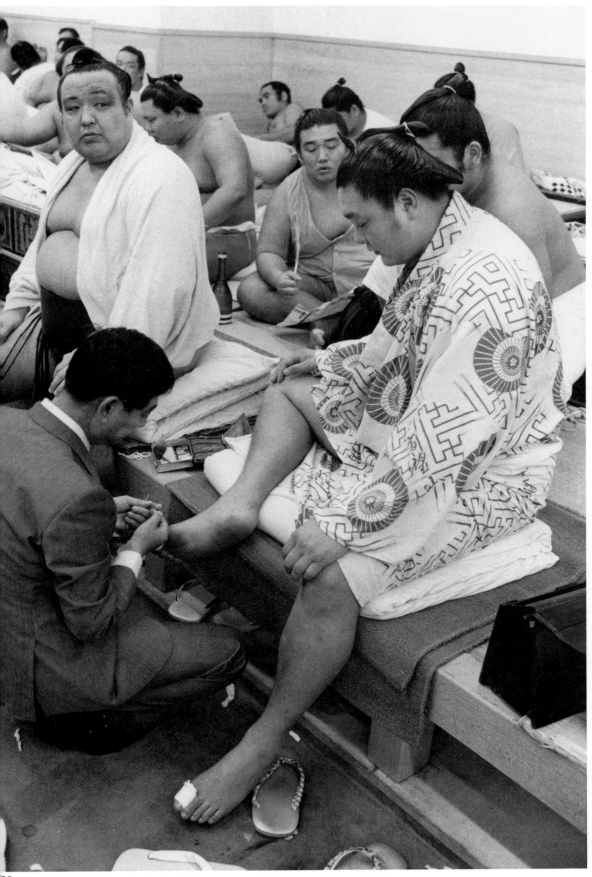

51

協会関係者以外
立入禁止
一般の方は
入れません

非常口
EXIT

55

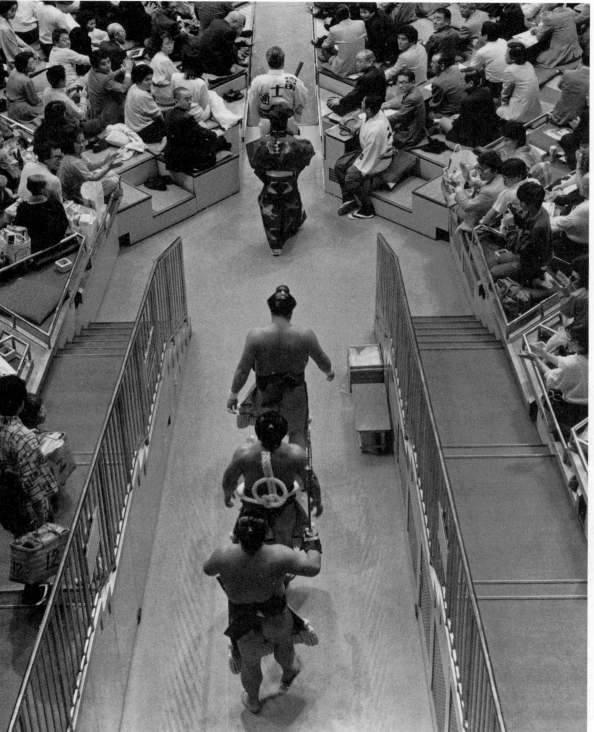

58

On the Road

Though three of the six annual tournaments are at the Kokugikan in Tokyo, the other three take place in the cities of Osaka, Nagoya, and Fukuoka. In addition, each tournament except the first of the year is followed by a regional tour, jungyo.

Jungyo means an enormous amount of organization and work, as the rikishi travel from town to town setting up camp, giving daily exhibition bouts, and then breaking camp and moving on again. The facilities available vary greatly, from local sports centers to high school gymnasiums to temporary outdoor rings. Morning keiko practice may be held under the open skies; a rikishi has his chommage groomed in a parking lot. During jungyo, everything is makeshift and uncomfortable. The younger rikishi, especially, are burdened with the extra chores, the lifting, toting, packing, and unloading that travel entails. But the rewards are undeniable: jungyo is a chance to experiment with new techniques without the risk of demotion, since these are exhibition matches and winning or losing doesn't affect the rikishi's standing. Just as important, the less formal atmosphere of the regional tournaments and the jungyo tours promotes warm contact with fans all over Japan and assures that the national sport will continue to reap the enthusiasm and support of future generations. Most rikishi are country boys; on the road, they have a chance to go home again.

63

64

68

69

71

73

74

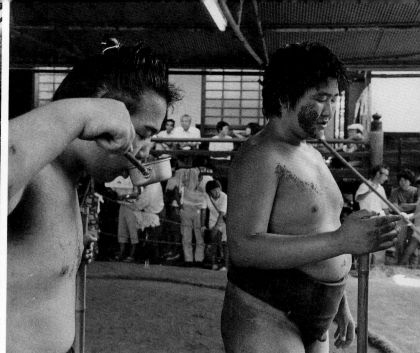

75

76

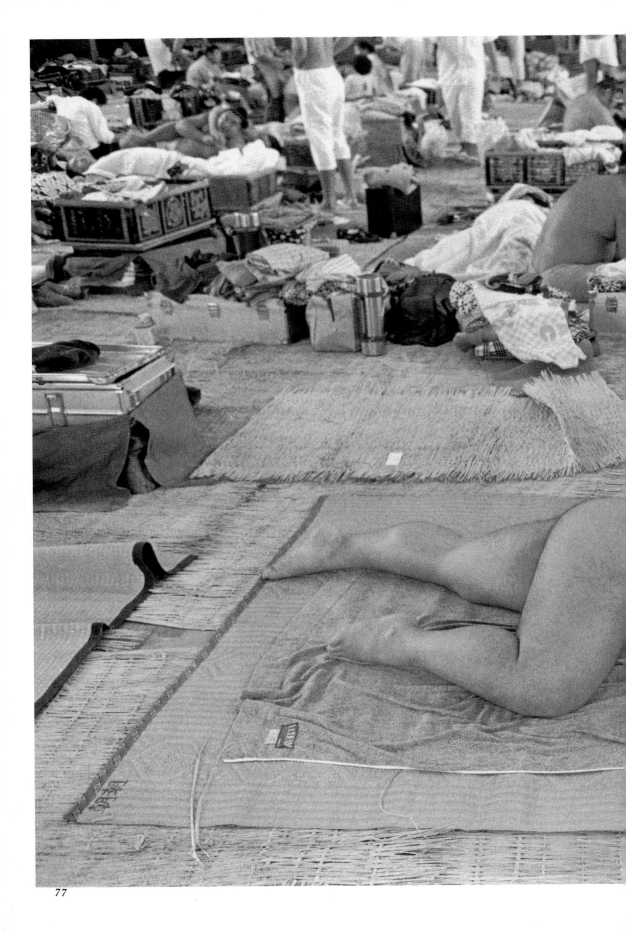

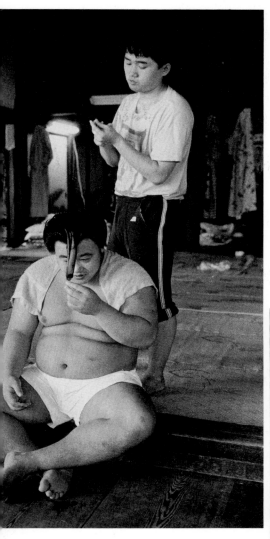

81

82

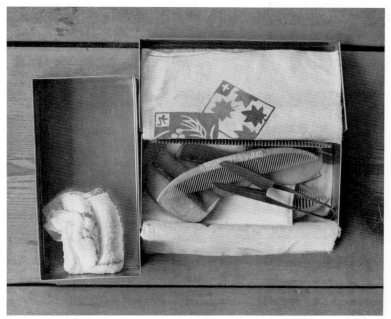

83

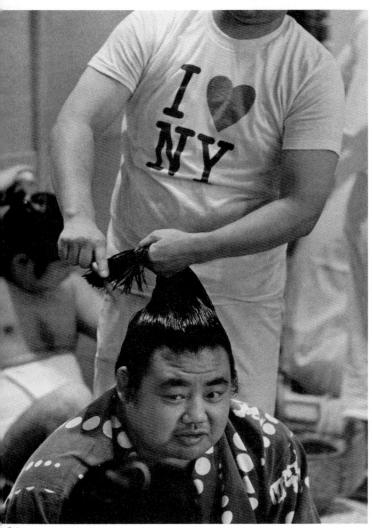

84

85

86

90

93

94

98

99

104

105

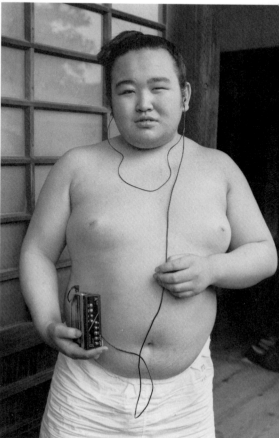

106

Public and Private

Does a rikishi have a private life? His very presence in modern Japan is a performance—his enormous bulk, his gleaming chommage, and his kimono make a statement just by being there. He understands this and chooses to devote much of the time he is not in the ring to public causes—school visits, promoting fire and police safety drives, guest appearances on television. In some ways, the most private of his life's moments are the most public. A high-ranking rikishi's wedding, for example, is a national celebration. The most public events may, in turn, be the most private: the same rikishi's retirement ceremony, when his chommage is cut off before the watching Kokugikan audience, remains in a special way his own inviolable moment as the memories of his long career run through his mind.

Where is the rikishi at home? In the heya, surrounded by his fellow athletes, to whom he is a friend, not a symbol. That is where he can truly relax and play a game of cards, put together a puzzle, compose a tune, watch a favorite TV program. The Ryogoku area, because so many sumo heya are concentrated there, provides a neighborhood sanctuary, too, a sort of extension of the heya. There, in a coffee shop, pachinko parlor, or game center, he can forget for a moment his public role.

109

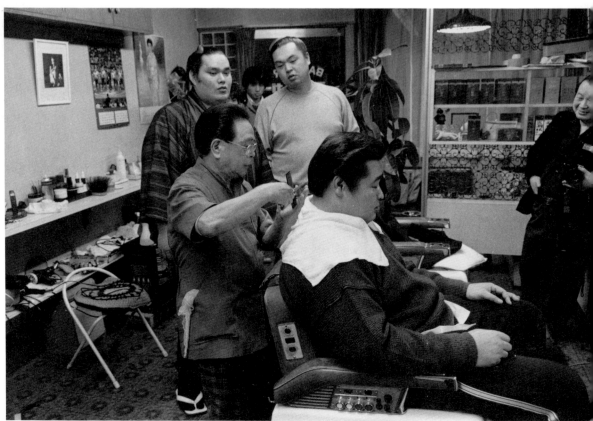

110

113

114

115

116

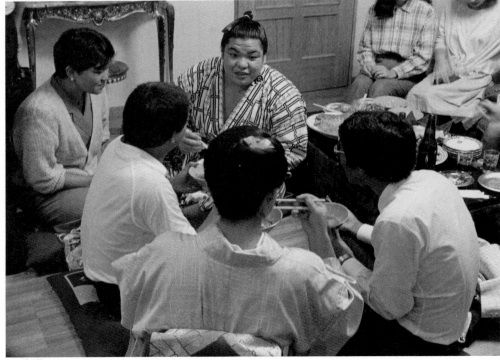

117

118

119

ハンバーガー

サンデイーヌ	¥260	シーフード	¥300
ミックス	¥270	ジャンボ	¥300
チーズ	¥330	デラックス	¥340
フィッシュ	¥340		
チキン	¥320		
チキンてりやき	¥340		

ミックスバーガー
フィッシュバーガー

127

128

130

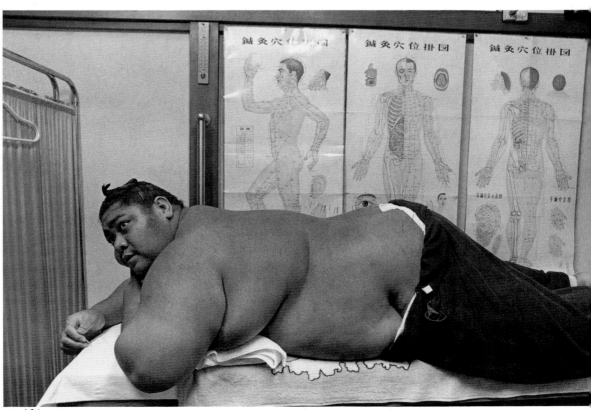

131

133

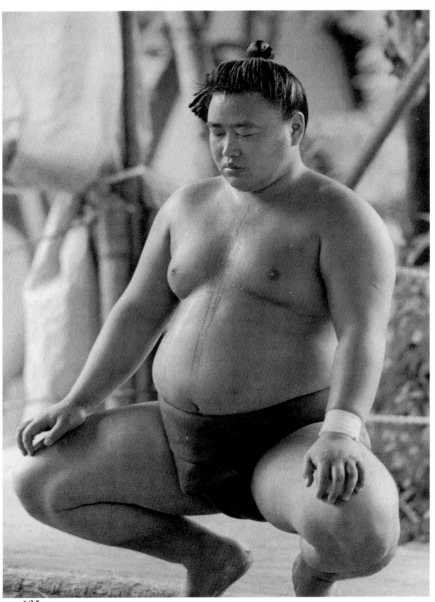

135

Captions

HEYA LIFE

1. Hair awry, a young rikishi squats into position in the practice ring at his heya and readies for the charge.

2. While one rikishi braces himself, a younger one prepares to rush him and attempt to push him back to the other side of the ring. Above the windows at the rear hang wooden plaques with the names of the rikishi in the heya arranged by order of rank.

3. Young rikishi look on as two of their number are locked in combat.

4. Keiko practice provides rikishi a chance to hone their skills and learn from observing others. While waiting for one's turn, there's also time for strengthening the arms with weights.

5—6. At 6:30 A.M., in a very cold, unheated room, rikishi try to get themselves going for the long keiko session ahead.

7. One rikishi holds a basket of salt for the senior rikishi, who each throw some into the ring to purify it—for salt is a purifier in the native Japanese religion, Shinto. The rikishi in the foreground squats in the traditional sumo *shiko* exercise for stretching and strengthening leg muscles.

8—9. In an alley behind Oshima beya, space is made for an outdoor "gym." Some rikishi supplement time-honored sumo exercises with weight training.

10. Oyakata and neighborhood people look on as young rikishi are paced through rigorous leg-stretching exercises. The oyakata holds a *shinai,* the split-bamboo staff he uses to discipline and direct his rikishi.

11. Ozeki Kitao gives a stroke of encouragement to a young member of the heya.

12. The oyakata supervises morning keiko sessions, observing the rikishis' progress and contemplating their prospects. The shinai is always close by.

13. With the experience of years in the ring to draw on, the oyakata

demonstrates a move from the side-lines during keiko.

14. In Tatsunami beya, after a long practice session, the rikishi meditate for several minutes in a squatting position.

15. Straw brooms sweep the practice ring after keiko. An aesthetic of simplicity, cleanliness, and purity is an inteqral part of sumo.

16. From huge pots of chanko nabe to rotund stomachs to rice bowls and top-knots, there are no hard lines in sumo.

17. The oyakata's wife is the only woman inside the sumo family. She must be a mother, teacher, advisor, and confidant to the many young rikishi separated from their families and far from their home towns.

18. Preparing the chanko nabe begins early. Here *gobo,* a fibrous root, is be-ing cut into thin slivers. Rikishi naturally develop excellent kitchen skills over the years.

19. A young rikishi helps himself to the last bits of chanko. Rikishi eat in

order of rank, and by the time the juniors get their chance, the pickings may grow slim.

20. Young rikishi gather around the chanko for the morning meal with healthy appetites after their three-hour keiko practice.

21. Outside the heya, a young rikishi airs a mawashi over a convenient fence. Rikishi in the makushita divi-sion and below wear the same type of mawashi for practice and tour-naments. They are black or dark blue and measure forty-six centimeters in width and from six to nine meters in length. Sekitori wear white mawashi for practice and larger, often colorfully dyed mawashi for tournaments.

22. The entire heya is cleaned every morning. Against the background of the now peaceful ring, a rikishi runs up and down the wood floors wiping them with a cloth.

23. Rikishi and tokoyama meet daily to maintain the chommage. This view from the far side of the ring of the practice room shows the tokonoma, or alcove, in which works of art are

placed. The oyakata sits with his back to the tokonoma while observing keiko. To the left of the tokonoma is the heya shrine, or *kamidana,* hung with a sacred *shimenawa* rope similar to that worn by the yokozuna in the portrait on the adjacent wall. The hanging scroll reads *mu,* or nothingness, and the motto above the hairdresser encourages diligence and harmony.

24. The pleasures of seniority. While being massaged, a rikishi enjoys the morning paper.

25. Ozeki Kitao at work on his portable word processor during a quiet moment in his room in the heya.

26. Konishiki and his tsukebito pass some time in a shared hobby, jigsaw puzzles.

27. Catnaps after meals are a complement to vigorous training and just as important for putting on weight.

28. Yokozuna Chiyonofuji relaxes with a volume of poetry while getting the full attention of his hairdresser and tsukebito. The yokozuna's name is emblazoned on the large fan; the stuffed wolf's head echoes Chiyonofuji's nickname, "The Wolf." The portrait of three yokozuna hanging near the ceiling features Chiyonofuji in the center flanked by Kitanoumi and Takanosato.

29. Young rikishi are required to attend the Sumo Kyokai School where they study subjects such as sumo history, calligraphy, reading, and singing, including the traditional sumo songs called *jinku.*

30. Looking out the window, Kototenzan (John Tenta, a Canadian rikishi) seems underwhelmed by it all. He later left the sumo world, in July 1986, to become a professional wrestler. The strictures of sumo's tradition are difficult for many Westerners to accept for long.

31—33. In the days preceding the New Year's tournament, the traditional rope (*tsuna*) worn by the yokozuna is assembled by members of the heya. It is twisted from three strands. Each of them is made from hemp with a wire core. They are wrapped in white cotton and anchored to a pillar in the heya for the twisting. The rikishi wear white and red head-bands, white gloves, and white aprons for the ceremony, which takes place with much enthusiastic shouting and, often, to the accompaniment of flutes and drums.

34. It takes seven strong rikishi to tie the rope around the yokozuna.

35. Traditional announcements (ban-zuke) of the upcoming tournament are sent out from every heya to friends, neighbors, and relatives, a task that falls to the young rikishi. Many local shops in the Ryogoku area display banzuke in their windows.

36. Colorful *sagari,* the hanging fringes that decorate the senior rikishi's mawashi, need to be carefully braided and starched. These often fall off during the first few seconds of fighting.

37. Hand prints and signatures of popular rikishi are layed out to dry in the heya.

38. *Zoni,* a traditional soup eaten on

New Year's morning, is served to all the rikishi as well as friends and neighbors who visit that day.

39. *Mochi* is another New Year's dish. It is made by pounding a special glutinous rice into a doughy paste. Mochi made by rikishi is thought to be particularly good because of the generous supply of manpower available for pounding it into a smooth consistency. Making the New Year's mochi is a felicitous ceremonial occasion, and as symbols of strength, vigor, and sound health, well-known rikishi are frequently called on to lend an auspicious hand to the task.

40. A rikishi stands under the shrine which can be seen in all heya. In the shape of a miniature Shinto shrine, it is decorated with a shimenawa, folded paper streamers (*gohei*), and sprigs of *sakaki,* a sacred tree. The oyakata and rikishi often bow to the shrine to pray for success and freedom from in-juries.

41. Members of Kokonoe beya gather for a brief ceremony to sanctify the practice ring prior to the New Year's tournament.

The Tournament

42. In the heat of a bout ozeki Wakashimazu lifts the much heavier ozeki Asashio entirely off the ground. The gyoji (referee), in his colorful traditional kimono, keeps an eye on the action, as do the five judges seated on the four sides of the ring (recognizable by the black haori they are wearing over their kimono). Rikishi awaiting their bouts are seated facing each other on the "East" and "West" sides (traditional divisions that don't correspond to the compass in the Ryogoku Kokugikan). Chiyonofuji and Asahifuji face the camera, on left and right.

43. Many of the shops on the streets of Ryogoku, the neighborhood where the great majority of heya are located, display signs featuring the figures of rikishi to advertise their products. A rikishi makes his way back home after a long day at the Kokugikan passing banners with a rikishi motif advertising a brand of rice cracker.

44. A few minutes of relaxation on the train platform.

45. Ozeki Wakashimazu stretches and limbers up using the practice pole unique to sumo. The pole also serves as a steadfast opponent for slapping or shoving with the shoulders.

46. Kotogaume seems confident that he will meet with success in the ring today.

47. A few minutes before his bout, Sasshunada receives an intense rub-down from one tsukebito to relieve the pre-bout tension that inevitably builds up, while another holds up his sagari, which are tucked into the mawashi.

48. Terao practices his starting position and eye contact, crucial to winning a match, in the shitaku beya.

49. With the assistance of a young tsukebito, the tokoyama shaves the rikishi's crown to form the traditional chommage topknot.

50. Just before his match, Asahifuji's acupuncturist treats him in the shitaku beya.

51. The shitaku beya is divided into East and West sides. For all the activity, the atmosphere is remarkably quiet. All thoughts are on the bout ahead, those few crucial moments in the ring.

52. Ozeki Kitao, one of the tallest men is sumo, practices a lunge to the throat of his tsukebito.

53. Not all rikishi are huge, nor are they especially fat. Many develop muscular physiques before putting on weight. No matter how large they become, they constantly practice to remain flexible and fast.

54. Konishiki banters with Asahifuji while their fans enjoy a close look at two young stars of sumo.

55. Wearing their decorative kesho mawashi, the rikishi wait for their entrance to the ring. Azumazeki oyakata, the ex-Takamiyama, stands above, looking toward the dohyo.

56. While the rikishi of one side parade around the dohyo in their ring-entering ceremony, the rikishi of the other side wait in the wings. They come into close contact with their fans as they press up the aisle.

57. The rikishi file into the ring.

58. The yokozuna has a special ring-entering ceremony after the makuuchi ceremony. The elaborate knot of the white yokozuna rope Chiyonofuji wears stands out dramatically. He is accompanied by two attendants, a "dew sweeper" (tsuyu harai) and sword bearer (tachimochi).

59. A close-up of the makuuchi ring-entering ceremony.

60. Chiyonofuji is surrounded by the press corps moments after winning a tournament, while his tokoyama rearranges his chommage. He will appear in the ring again in a few moments for the extended awards ceremony held on the last day of the tournament.

61. Covered with sand from a defeat on the dohyo, a rikishi removes his bandages and hopes for a better day tomorrow.

62. Terao relaxes with some light reading while waiting for a local train on the jungyo tour.

63. Rikishi gather at Tokyo Station to catch a bullet train that will take them to a destination on their jungyo tour.

64. The rikishi arrive at a jungyo site in Toyama, packing a local train station.

65. Cueing for taxis to take them to their lodgings, rikishi on jungyo stay at a different inn in every city.

66. Special trains are reserved to transport traveling rikishi. Local trains are slow and offer a good chance to catch up on sleep missed during the busy jungyo schedule.

67. Sumo posters cover the doors of the tournament hall in Nagoya. Fans already inside peer back outside toward the shitaku beya entrance, hoping to catch a glimpse of the arriving rikishi.

68. Rikishi manpower at work. All the cooking and kitchen supplies are packed up and moved to the next location by trucks, while the rikishi travel by train or bus.

69. Ozeki Asashio's luggage shares a seat with his tukebito on an already crowded bus.

70. In every town on the jungyo tour, local people gather around the sumo camp to get a firsthand look at their heroes. The temporary scaffolding will eventually form part of an outdoor "stadium."

71. A practice ring is built during tournaments outside of Tokyo, too, and, just as in the heya, it is swept clean at the end of the daily keiko session, salt is thrown out from the edge to the center, and Shinto streamers, gohei, are inserted there.

72. A rikishi wipes off sand and sweat after a long morning keiko.

73. Despite their size, seasoned rikishi can easily perform leg splits

and other feats that require extreme flexibility. This young rikishi begins the long training process with the help of one of his fellows.

74. The oyakata reprimands two young rikishi for having spoken during practice. During keiko, the less said the better.

75. A scoop of water to rinse out the mouth during the morning session.

76. An early morning warm-up in an open field during jungyo. Later in the day the matches will be held at the local sports center.

77. Ozeki Asashio naps. The bottle at his side is popular among senior rikishi as a water vessel.

78—80. Rikishi and tokoyama meet several times during the day to groom the chommage. There's usually enough time to read a comic or the sports news during the tokoyama's attentions.

81—82. Everything is makeshift and uncomfortable during jungyo.

83. The tokoyama's kit of traditional wooden combs and clippers.

84. Ozutsu gets his chommage straightened and cleaned.

85. Whether traveling or at the home heya, the hearty meals cooked daily require quite a cleanup operation. The intimacy created by sharing all of these activities—shopping, cooking, eating, and washing up—over the years contributes greatly to the bonds that grow among the rikishi of the same heya.

86. A friendly meeting of rikishi and fans in a small town. What do you say to your hero? A smile of admiration is enough.

87. Fresh shrimp from the morning market, destined for that day's tempura.

88. Konishiki is visited by a group of baseball-capped sumo fans during a school excursion.

89. During the Nagoya tournament, Hoshi talks with a patron after the evening meal. Being a senior rikishi,

Hoshi is entitled to a private room in the large temple where the rikishi are staying.

90—91. Tegata are a major chore for famous rikishi. Hundreds can be made in assembly-line fashion.

92. On *senshuraku*, the last day of the tournament, everyone is busy sorting and packing for the move to the next location.

93—94. A young rikishi carefully irons and wraps an under kimono for his senior.

95. The mawashi is hung out to dry on a scaffoldlike clothesline outside the temple where the rikishi are staying.

96—97. The simplest chores go to the youngest rikishi.

98. While conversing on the phone, Chiyonofuji has his back fanned during the hot and humid Nagoya tournament.

99. Chiyonofuji is assisted with his obi before leaving to meet some sponsors for a drink.

100. At six o'clock in the morning, rikishi help each other put on the long mawashi.

101. Twenty or thirty rikishi sleep in the main room of a temple during the Nagoya tournament.

102. Visitors often bring babies to the temple or heya hoping a rikishi—possibly even a yokozuna—will pick them up and allow himself to be photographed with them, which would mean very good luck.

103. Ozeki Onokuni administers a playful headlock to one of his tsukebito.

104. Relaxing with some light reading.

105. With waxed hair not quite long enough to form into a chommage, a young rikishi makes his way to the tournament.

106. The traditional lifestyle of the rikishi does not exclude the latest in electronics.

107. All dohyo are sacred and

therefore require special attention and maintenance. The temporary dohyo used during regional tournaments must be broken up on the last day since it can no longer be properly cared for.

PUBLIC AND PRIVATE

108. Fujizakura in his retirement ceremony at the Kokugikan. The chommage is cut off in small increments by sumo officials, friends, and fellow rikishi. The final cut is made by his senior oyakata.

109. Most retiring rikishi don't make the top ranks and have their hair-cutting ceremony at the heya.

110. Immediately after the chommage is cut, the rikishi goes for his first modern haircut in many years. His friends from the heya look on and wonder, "Am I next?"

111. Oyakata Azumazeki, popularly known as Jesse, occasionally looks at the chommage he wore for over twenty years before retiring. It is kept on display in a glass case in his home.

112. On jungyo, local kids in mawashi participate in the show by taking on famous rikishi. Kitao is in the ring, with Chiyonofuji and Asashio looking benevolently on.

113. Several well-known rikishi pair off with popular singers for duets on a televised fund-raising show after the New Year's tournament.

114. Retired yokozuna Kitanoumi (*right*) and Ozeki Asashio (*left*) visit a school where they answer students' questions ("What did you eat when you were a kid?") and give advice ("Study hard, listen to your mom, and always try your best").

115. Ozeki Asashio and his bride "break" the sake barrel at their wedding party, attended by fifteen hundred people, as Onokuni, Hokutenyu, and Chiyonofuji look on. Sumo weddings are often opulent affairs enjoyed

by the entire country through the mass media.

116—17. Yokozuna Chiyonofuji (*above*) and Hoshi (*below*) relax at a gathering of friends and patrons hosted by their oyakata on the night after the tournament's closing day.

118—19. At an inn on tour. (*above*) One rikishi winds a *haramaki* (''belly band'') around his middle while the other relaxes with a call home. (*below*) In the tub.

120. Rikishi fill a local public bathhouse in a small town.

121. Stopping for some burgers on the way back home from the shitaku beya.

122. A quick bowl of noodles in the restaurant at the Kokugikan before heading home.

123. A rikishi settles into a seat at a pachinko parlor, haven for fans of the pinball-like amusement popular for its transcendental qualities.

124. The chommage holds down a bill during a traditional card game called *hanafuda*.

125. After some morning grocery shopping, a quick stop at a cafe for a change of pace: coffee, toast, eggs, and a cigarette.

126. Time out for the latest version of space invaders when the day's work is completed.

127. Two or three rikishi from each heya meet at the local supermarket to pick up the day's supplies.

128. A shop in Ryogoku carries especially large sizes for rikishi.

129. Checking out the local produce in an open market during the Nagoya tournament.

130. Relaxing rikishi engrossed in the antics of a pro wrestling match on TV.

131. Konishiki receives his acupuncture treatment at a small clinic in Asakusabashi where several famous rikishi go.

132. Many rikishi are musically

talented. Here one composes on a portable keyboard.

133—34. The bamboo shinai is the unofficial bat, and a ball is made from yards of used adhesive tape for a back-alley game of baseball.

135. A rikishi in meditation, sweating from a long morning workout, an image that encompasses his dedication to the sport and the life of sumo.

by Joel Sackett

APPENDICES

Appendix I: Tournaments

There are six annual basho (official fifteen-day tournaments) held on a regular seasonal schedule, though the exact dates vary a few days each year. The first tournament is the New Years' or Hatsu Basho, held at the Kokugikan in Ryogoku, Tokyo, from mid-January. This is followed by the Osaka Basho, held at the Osaka Sports Stadium in March. Sumo returns to Tokyo in May for the Haru or Spring Basho, again at the Kokugikan in Ryogoku. The Natsu or Summer Basho is held in Nagoya at the Aichi Gymnasium in July. In September, Tokyo's Kokugikan is the site of the Aki (Autumn) Basho. The year closes with the Hakata Basho, held at Fukuoka Sun Plaza in November.

Tickets for a basho go on sale approximately six weeks before the tournament, but several hundred tickets for seats in the upper balconies are reserved and sold each day at reasonable prices. You have to get in line early.

For those in Japan with the urge to travel, jungyo, or countryside tours, provide a unique opportunity to see sumo on the road. Jungyo takes place after each tournament except the Hatsu Basho. Jungyo destinations and dates vary every year, and the schedule can be learned by calling (in Japanese) the Sumo Kyokai at (03) 623-5111 or the Sumo Kyokai Jungyo Bu, the department specifically in charge of the tours, at (03) 625-6565.

Appendix II: Ranks

All rikishi are ranked in one of six divisions, which are explained below in order of descending rank. During a tournament, rikishi are further divided into East and West sides, the East being favored and its rikishi taking precedence over those on the West.

Makuuchi (or Makunouchi) Division.   There are five ranks within the Makuuchi Division. *Makuuchi* means "within the curtain," referring to the custom during the feudal period of allowing the higher-ranking wrestlers to sit with the shogun behind a curtain near the ring. At the top of the Makuuchi Division is the *yokozuna,* sometimes called grand champion in English. Generally there are from one to four yokozuna, but there can be more or even none. This highest rank is awarded according to merit, as determined by the Sumo Kyokai. While poor performance can result in the demotion of rikishi of other ranks, a yokozuna remains a yokozuna until his retirement from the sport, which is the only route open to a yokozuna who can no longer perform to the standards of sumo's highest position.

Next in the Makuuchi Division are the *ozeki,* often called champions. There are usually two or more, but there have been none at times, in which case the yokozuna in referred to as yokozuna-ozeki. There can be four or more ozeki at one time as well. After the ozeki come the *sekiwake,* or junior champions. Their number is set: one on the East side and one on the West. Next are the *komusubi,* junior champions, second rank. Again, there is one each on East and West. The last rank in the Makuuchi Division is the *maegashira,* often called senior rikishi. There are normally thirteen or fourteen on both East and West, for a total of from twenty-six to twenty-eight. When there are not enough rikishi deemed qualified for this rank, the numbers on each side are reduced one by one, West before East.

A collective term, *sanyaku,* (three ranks) is used to refer to the ozeki, sekiwake, and komusubi.

Juryo Division.   The Juryo Division is sometimes translated as Contenders, but the name means "ten pieces of gold," which was the payment received by the rikishi in this division long ago. To this day, the Juryo Division is the first rank in which the rikishi receive a regular salary of any size. There are normally thirteen Juryo rikishi on East and West, for a total of twenty-six.

Makushita Division.   Sometimes called Second Class, *makushita* means "outside the curtain." There are 60 Makushita wrestlers on both East and West, making a total of 120.

Sandamme Division. *Sandamme* refers to the third line from the bottom on the sumo listing, which is where the names of these rikishi appear. There can be up to two hundred Sandamme rikishi, and it usually takes a long time to travel up through the division.

Jonidan Division. The "Second Step Up From the Bottom" is a giant division that may include as many as 300 wrestlers, but normally there are from 270 to 280 rikishi, that number divided between East and West.

Jonokuchi Division. This is the "First Step" into the ranks of the rikishi. There are normally seventy-eight in the Jonokuchi Division, but the number can vary. Before entering this division, fledgling rikishi are called *maezumo,* or "before sumo."

A rikishi may rise or fall through the ranks according to his performance in the preceding tournament. Though it varies from case to case and all ranking decisions are determined by the Sumo Kyokai, usually a majority of losses (called *makekoshi*) makes a rikishi liable to demotion, so the race to rack up a majority of victories (*kachikoshi*) is keen. (With an odd number of bouts there are no even scores.) New rankings are issued two weeks prior to the upcoming basho. These are all written in a traditional style of calligraphy on the large board called the banzuke that is then photographed and printed. The size of the writing becomes smaller and smaller as the list reaches the lower ranks. The referees and sumo officials are also listed according to their rankings. Oyakata are listed, too, ranked by their position in the Sumo Kyokai.

Only the Makuuchi and Juryo rikishi have bouts on each day of the fifteen-day tournament. The other rikishi have seven bouts. Makuuchi and Juryo rikishi wear silk mawashi and all others wear coarsely woven black mawashi. Colored mawashi for the top two divisions came into fashion with color television broadcasts of the tournaments. Ex-yokozuna Kitanofuji, who is known for his fashionable style, was the first to wear a colored mawashi. Purists like the present yokozuna Chiyonofuji still insist on wearing only black mawashi.

Appendix III: Koen Kai

Newspapers and magazines often mention the koen kai (fan clubs) for the different heya and sekitori, but little is ever explained about how to join, become active in the club, and get to know the rikishi. It is not difficult, and several koen kai include non-Japanese members, both male and female. The best route is to write a letter (in Japanese) to the oyakata or sekitori expressing your desire to join. Letters to the sekitori can be sent in care of the heya to which he belongs. The parties held by the koen kai once or twice a year are fun to attend, and the cost is not prohibitive. Those who join will also receive the banzuke before each tournament and a periodic present from the heya or sekitori.

Ajigawa
1–7–4 Mori
Koto-ku, Tokyo 135

Asahiyama
4–14–21 Kita Kasai
Edogawa-ku, Tokyo 134

Azumazeki
4–6–4 Higashi Komagata
Sumida-ku, Tokyo 130

Dewanoumi
2–3–15 Ryogoku
Sumida-ku, Tokyo 130

Fujishima
3–10–6 Honcho
Nakano-ku, Tokyo 164

Futagoyama
3–25–10 Narita Higashi
Suginami-ku, Tokyo 166

Hanaregoma
3–12–7 Asagaya Minami
Suginami-ku, Tokyo 166

Isegahama
5–7–14 Hakusan
Bunkyo-ku, Tokyo 112

Isenoumi
3–8–80 Harue-cho
Edogawa-ku, Tokyo 132

Izutsu
2–2–7 Ryogoku
Sumida-ku, Tokyo 130

Kagamiyama
8–16–1 Kita Koiwa
Edogawa-ku, Tokyo 133

Kasugano
1–7–11 Ryogoku
Sumida-ku, Tokyo 130

Kasugayama
1–10–14 Saga
Koto-ku, Tokyo 135

Kataonami
1–33–9 Ishiwara
Sumida-ku, Tokyo 130

Kise
2–35–21 Hongo
Bunkyo-ku, Tokyo 113

Kitanoumi
2–10–11 Kiyosumi
Koto-ku, Tokyo 135

Kokonoe
1–16–1 Kamezawa
Sumida-ku, Tokyo 130

Kumagatani
1–6–28 Minami Koiwa
Edogawa-ku, Tokyo 133

Magaki
3–8–1 Kamezawa
Sumida-ku, Tokyo 130

Michinoku
3–13–14 Hirai
Edogawa-ku, Tokyo 132

Mihogaseki
3–2–12 Chitose
Sumida-ku, Tokyo 130

Minato
2–20–10 Shibanakata
Kawaguchi-shi, Saitama-ken 333

Miyagino
4–16–3 Midori
Sumida-ku, Tokyo 130

Musashigawa
3–2–9 Hirano
Koto-ku, Tokyo 135

Nishonoseki
4–17–1 Ryogoku
Sumida-ku, Tokyo 130

Onaruto
2–22–14 Kitakata
Ichikawa-shi, Chiba-ken 272

Oshima
3–5–3 Ryogoku
Sumida-ku, Tokyo 130

Oshiogawa
2–17–7 Kiba
Koto-ku, Tokyo 135

Oyama
5–35–13 Higashi Koiwa
Edogawa-ku, Tokyo 133

Sadogatake
4–18–13 Taihei
Sumida-ku, Tokyo 130

Taiho
2–8–3 Kiyosumi
Koto-ku, Tokyo 135

Takadagawa
2–1–15 Ichinoe
Edogawa-ku, Tokyo 132

Takasago
1–22–5 Yanagibashi
Taito-ku, Tokyo 111

Tokitsukaze
3–15–3 Ryogoku
Sumida-ku, Tokyo 130

Tatsunami
3–26–2 Ryogoku
Sumida-ku, Tokyo 130

Tomozuna
1–20–7 Mori
Koto-ku, Tokyo 135

Tatsutagawa
4–7–11 Ryogoku
Sumida-ku, Tokyo 130

Wakamatsu
2–10–8 Ryogoku
Sumida-ku, Tokyo 130

Information on sumo is available (in Japanese) through the Japan Sumo Association at:

Nihon Sumo Kyokai
(Japan Sumo Association)
1–3–28 Yokoami
Sumida-ku, Tokyo 130
623–5111

Appendix IV: Chanko Nabe

That wonderful, aromatic, stew-type meal eaten daily by the sumo world can be made from any fish, meat, or fowl—or sometimes a combination of these—plus plenty of fresh vegetables. The following two recipes were taken down in the kitchen of Kokonoe beya, the heya of yokozuna Chiyonofuji. They make enough chanko nabe to feed thirty rikishi, and two or three large pots (*nabe*) are required to prepare this amount. I have given each recipe just as it's made in the heya to give an idea of the volume of food prepared for one meal there, but the recipes are very flexible, and the portions can easily be reduced to a more practical amount for your home. In reducing the recipes, it's important to remember that a simple calculation of the amount per guest will still result in too much food: your guests and family may not eat the quantities of food that the three-hundred to four-hundred-pound rikishi do. Metric measurements are provided with approximate English equivalents in parentheses.

WHITE FISH CHANKO NABE

This is a simple and delicate-tasting stew that is served with *ponzu,* or lightly vinegared sauce.

Ingredients

Chanko:

2 pots containing 4 liters (1 gallon) of boiling water each
20 kilos (44 pounds) of fresh nonflaky white fish, cleaned and scaled. Leave
   bones and head intact and cut into 3-centimeter (1-inch) chunks
10 cakes of fresh tofu (bean curd)
2 or 3 large heads of *hakusai* (Chinese cabbage)
3 large *negi* (a mild type of leek)
5 large bunches of fresh spinach, about 250 grams (8 ounces) each
4 kilos (9 pounds) of fresh, drained bean sprouts (*moyashi*)

Ponzu Sauce (for thirty rikishi):

Ponzu, which often contains citrus juice as well, can also be purchased ready-made at most Oriental food stores.

2 liters (2 quarts) of *dashi* (stock that can be made from instant powder now
  available around the world at specialty stores)
25 to 30 cc (¼ cup) of rice vinegar (not regular Western-style vinegar, as it is
  too strong in flavor)
2 or 3 tablespoons of Japanese soy sauce

The portions can be adjusted to taste, but it should not be too strong or you
will kill the wonderful delicate taste of the stew itself.

Note: It is important to remember that you don't cook all the above at once,
but start with one-quarter of the total ingredients divided into the two pots of
boiling water. The chanko nabe tastes better as it cooks and fresh ingredients
are added as the cooked ones are eaten.

Start by adding the fish tails, fins, and other inedible parts of the fish. Boil slowly for 15
to 20 minutes and remove fish parts and skim off the foam. The balance of the cooking
is normally done at the table, but it can be done in the kitchen and served with a hot
plate under the pot at the table. The guests must dip into the pot with a ladle and serve
themselves.

First add about 1/3 of the remaining fish and let simmer for 10 minutes before adding
the vegetables, which have all been cut into bite-size pieces, except for the spinach,
which is left in its original form and put in as it is needed, since it cooks so quickly.

At each place, set a deep soup bowl with about 2 ½ tablespoons of the ponzu in it.
Each person serves himself from the cooking pot, dipping his serving into the ponzu
before eating it. Serve with 13 kilos (29 pounds, measured before cooking) of plain boiled rice in separate, individual bowls, and Japanese pickles.

This is a healthy and very enjoyable meal. If you are watching your weight, forgo the
rice! Beer or sake go well with this chanko nabe, and a dry white wine can also be enjoyed with it.

BUTA MISO CHANKO NABE

This is an equally easy meal to fix, but the ingredients are more complicated and
numerous. All should be available, however, at your local butcher or any oriental food
specialty shop (or the gourmet section of the local supermarket).

Ingredients

instant *dashi,* enough for 4 liters (1 gallon; see preceding recipe)

3 packages miso (fermented bean paste; a combination of light and dark miso
is preferred)

soy sauce and sake to taste

10 kilos (22 pounds) of thinly sliced fresh pork (the shoulder cut with some fat
is best)

1 large daikon (large white radish that is mild in flavor)

4 large carrots

10 peeled onions

2 large heads of cabbage

5 packs of *konnyaku* (a gelatinous substance made from a wild mountain
vegetable. If not available, it won't be missed)

30 *shiitake* (fresh brown Japanese mushrooms—dried can be used, but first they
should be soaked overnight and drained)

10 *aburaage* (fried tofu cakes, frequently available in frozen form outside Japan)

Take 2 large nabe and put 2 liters (2 quarts) of dashi (see preceding recipe) in each. Mix in the equivalent of three packages of miso (bean paste) using a combination of the light (slightly sweet) and dark miso. Add a small amount of soy sauce and sake to taste. Bring to a simmer.

First add the vegetables that take a long time to cook (all cut in bite-size pieces) such as the carrots, daikon, onions, and part of the cabbage. Then add the shiitake and part of the meat. Keep adding as the ingredients are eaten.

Serve, as in the above recipe, with 13 kilos (29 pounds) of plain boiled rice, Japanese pickles, and thin omelettes filled with chopped meat or vegetables. This is truly delicious and perhaps a taste you have never had before. Enjoy this with beer, sake, or a dry white wine.

If the above sounds too much for you to tackle at home, or you feel the need to do a little first-hand research before getting started, try one of the chanko nabe restaurants in the Asakusabashi or Ryogoku areas. If you are in Japan, look for the advertisements of chanko nabe restaurants in *Sumo World,* the excellent English-language magazine on sumo. Two especially recommended restaurants in Tokyo are:

Kitaseumi Chanko
1-21-22 Nishi Koiwa
Edogawa-ku
Tel: (03) 672-7393

Chanko Tomoegata
2-17 Ryogoku
Sumida-ku
Tel: (03) 632-5600

Both of these establishments and most chanko restaurants will serve one or more persons, and parties are welcome. (Telephone in advance for large groups, however.) Chanko Tomoegata has the advantage of an illustrated menu.

The more the merrier when eating chanko nabe, so take some friends with you on this adventure. Remember, the more guests eating from the pot, the bigger it will be and the more ingredients it will include.

Glossary of Sumo Terms

Banzuke. The list of rankings issued by the Sumo Kyokai two weeks prior to a tournament. It is written in old-style Japanese characters by a referee and then photographed and printed on Japanese paper. The higher-ranking rikishi appear in the upper portion, descending in order of rank. Judges, referees, and other members of the Sumo Kyokai also appear on the banzuke. The writing grows smaller and smaller as the rankings become lower until a magnifying glass is almost needed to read the bottom listings.

Basho. Literally, "the location," it refers to the six tournaments conducted each year, three in Tokyo (in January, May, and September) and one each in Osaka (March), Nagoya (July), and Fukuoka or Hakata (November). A basho lasts fifteen days, starting and ending on a Sunday.

Chommage. The distinctive topknot that is associated with the sumo rikishi today.

Dohyo. The ring in which the sumo match takes place. It is made from pounded clay and its boundary is marked by a circle of rice-straw bales representing the buried bales of rice used in sumo of an earlier day. For tournaments, a two-foot-high mound is built, but in the heya, the dohyo is flat, though the size of the circle is always the same: fifteen feet in diameter. The surface of the dohyo is covered with a thin layer of sand.

Dohyo Iri. The ring-entering ceremony performed by the sekitori before the start of their division's bouts. The rikishi of the Juryo Division, for example, first enter the dohyo divided into East and West sides, with each rikishi stepping up onto the dohyo wearing a colorful apron (see *kesho mawashi*) as his name is called by an announcer (*yobidashi*). The announcer also gives the rikishi's rank, home prefecture, and heya. After all the rikishi have been announced, they face into the circle and perform a short series of ritual gestures before filing out of the ring and leaving down the aisles. The process is repeated for the Makuuchi Division, and finally the yokozuna come out one at a time to perform their special dohyo iri. They are accompanied by two attendant rikishi, and the yokozuna dohyo iri is longer and more complicated than that for other rikishi.

Gyoji. The referee, easily recognized by his colorful traditional costume and hat. The gyoji are ranked as well, with higher-ranking gyoji officiating at the bouts of higher-ranking rikishi.

Heya. Frequently translated as "stable," this term refers to a group within the sumo world as well as to the place where they live and train. Rikishi from the same heya do not compete against each other unless they are tied for the winning position, or *yusho,* of their division on the last day of the tournament.

Jungyo. Literally, a tour of the countryside or provinces. Sumo jungyo takes place after each of the basho except for the first one of the year, in January, when it is too cold. Over two hundred men from the sumo world, including rikishi of all ranks, gyoji, and oyakata, travel together putting on exhibition bouts for the public. Extensive keiko (practice) sessions are held each morning, and the public is permitted to watch.

Juryo. See Appendix II.

Keiko. Sumo practice. It is also a warming up and general exercise period that is generally supervised by the oyakata.

Kesho Mawashi. The colorful apronlike garment worn by the Juryo- and Makuuchi-division rikishi when they perform the dohyo iri. It is normally presented to the sekitori by a sponsor or koen kai. Kesho mawashi are handwoven and are valued at well over ¥1,000,000 (about $6,000) each. The sekitori's name always appears on it, as does the name of the donor.

Koen Kai. The fan club for the heya or sekitori. There are many koen kai around the country, but the main ones are in Tokyo. See Appendix III.

Kokugikan. "Hall of the National Sport" —the sumo stadium where the Tokyo tournaments are conducted. The Kokugikan was built in 1984 and opened in January 1985. It is located near Ryogoku Station on the National Railways Sobu Line.

Sumo Kyokai. Generally referred to as the Sumo Professional Association, the Sumo Kyokai is the governing body of the sport and is composed of retired sekitori who own a share in the association. Shares (toshiyori kabu) are limited in number, and each carries a name, which is used by the individual after he retires and becomes an oyakata.

Makuuchi. See Appendix II.

Mawashi. The long belt that is wrapped around the waist and the stomach to the back, covering the private parts of the rikishi. It is made of heavy silk, the grade depending on the rank of the rikishi and the occasion. Black is the traditional color for mawashi, but today many rikishi wear other colors.

Oyakata. A retired sekitori who owns a

share (kabu) in the Sumo Kyokai. Also called a toshiyori (elder). The oyakata are responsible for the administration of the Sumo Kyokai and the sport in general. They also serve as trainers and heads of heya.

Rikishi. It has been the custom among English-language publications to refer to the participants in sumo as wrestlers, but this is not really an accurate term. The proper Japanese term is rikishi, and this refers to all ranks from the yokozuna on down.

Sekitori. Any rikishi who is in the Juryo or Makuuchi Division is called a sekitori. The term senior is used to refer to a rikishi who has privileges in the heya, and this can include individuals who have been in the heya for a long time but have not achieved the rank of sekitori. There are a variety of pecking orders in sumo, and seniority in daily life within the heya does not always depend on rank. Professional rank is, however, the ultimate determining factor, and sekitori are at the top of the ranking.

Shitaku Beya. "Room for preparations." This is the dressing room where the rikishi change and wait for their time to appear in the ring.

Sumotori. This refers to rikishi below the Juryo Division, in other words, those who do not qualify as sekitori.

Tegata. The hand print of a sekitori. Highly prized, they are normally made with red ink, but sometimes black ink is used. They are signed in black ink with a brush. Tegata are sold by the Sumo Kyokai during basho and jungyo, and the sekitori must donate their tegata to the Kyokai. In addition, tegata are made for sponsors and fans, in which case the sekitori are generally paid for their efforts. Tegata are usually on a square white piece of cardboard, but sometimes they are made on special Japanese paper as particularly prized gifts from the sekitori or the heya.

Tokoyama. The sumo hairdresser who is responsible for maintaining the chommage. There is an unofficial ranking among the tokoyama based on seniority, and only the senior tokoyama are allowed to dress the hair of a sekitori.

Toshiyori. See oyakata.

Tsukebito. Literally, servant or attendant. In sumo, all Juryo and Makuuchi rikishi have tsukebito, assigned from among the lower-ranking rikishi from the same heya. The higher the sekitori's rank the more tsukebito he has. Tsukebito are responsible for dressing and generally caring for the sekitori.

Yokozuna. See Appendix II.

-Zeki. An honorific suffix used when addressing or referring to any Juryo or Makuuchi rikishi by name, e.g., Chiyonofuji-zeki. Rikishi below the sekitori level are referred to with the standard honorific -san.

The "weathermark" identifies this book as a production of John Weatherhill, Inc., publishers of fine books on Asia and the Pacific. Editorial supervision: Jeffrey Hunter. Book design and typography: Miriam F. Yamaguchi. Layout of illustrations: Yutaka Shimoji. Production supervision: Mitsuo Okado. Composition of text: Yamagata Printing Co., Yokohama. Printing of text and engraving and printing of monochrome plates: Kyodo Printing Co., Tokyo. Binding: Makoto Binderies, Tokyo. The typeface used is Baskerville.

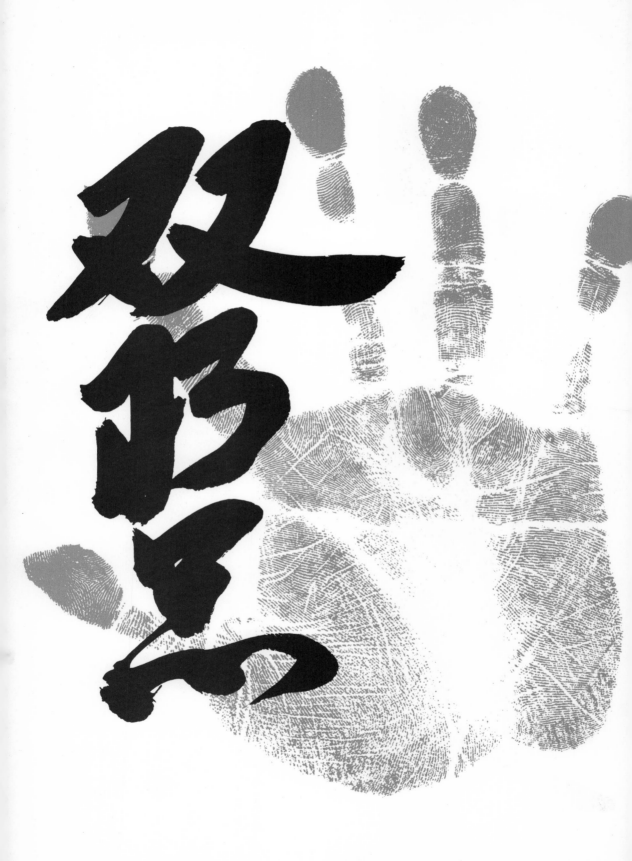